SEMIOTEXT(E) INTERVENTION SERIES

© The Invisible Committee, 2014.
This translation © 2015 by Semiotext(e).

Published by Semiotext(e)
PO BOX 629, South Pasadena, CA 91031
www.semiotexte.com

Special thanks to Noura Wedell.

Design: Hedi El Kholti

ISBN: 978-1-58435-167-2
Distributed by The MIT Press, Cambridge, Mass.
and London, England
Printed in the United States of America

The Invisible Committee

To Our Friends

Translated by Robert Hurley

semiotext(e)
intervention
series □ 18

Contents

To Billy, Guccio, Alexis, and
Jeremy Hammond then,

"There is no other world.
There's just another way to live."
— Jacques Mesrine

The insurrections have come, finally. At such a pace and in so many countries, since 2008, that the whole structure of this world seems to be disintegrating, piece by piece. Ten years ago, predicting an uprising would have exposed you to the snickers of the seated ones; now it's those who announce a return to order who make themselves look foolish. Nothing more solid, more self-assured, we were told, than the Tunisia of Ben Ali, the busy Turkey of Erdogan, social-democratic Sweden, Ba'athist Syria, Quebec on tranquilizers, or the Brazil of beaches, the *Bolsa Familia*, and peace-keeping police units. We've seen what followed. Stability is finished. In politics, too, they've learned to think twice before awarding a triple A.

An insurrection can erupt at any time, for any reason, and lead anywhere. The ruling politicians walk among the abysses. Their own shadows appear to threaten them. *¡Que se vayan todos!* was a slogan; it's become a common conviction, the *basso continuo* of the epoch, a rumble passing from voice to voice, then lifting up like an ax when it's least expected. The *cleverest* of the politicians have made it into a campaign promise. They don't have any choice. Incurable disgust, pure negativity, and absolute refusal are the only discernable political forces of the moment.

The insurrections have come, but not the revolution. Rarely has one seen, as we have these past few years, in such a densely-packed timespan, so many seats of power taken by storm, from Greece to Iceland. Occupying plazas in the very heart of cities, pitching tents there, erecting barricades, kitchens, or makeshift shelters, and holding assemblies will soon be part of the political reflex, like the strike used to be. It seems that the epoch has even begun to secrete its own platitudes, like that All Cops Are Bastards (ACAB) which a strange internationale emblazons on the rough walls of cities, from Cairo to Istanbul, and Rome to Paris or Rio, with every thrust of revolt.

But however great the disorders in this world may be, the revolution always seems to choke off at the riot stage. At best, a regime change satisfies for an instant the need to change the world, only to renew the same dissatisfaction. At worst, revolution serves as a stepping stone for those who speak in its name but only think of liquidating it. In places, France for example, the nonexistence of revolutionary forces with enough confidence in themselves clears the way for those whose profession is precisely to feign self-confidence, and offer it up as a spectacle: the fascists. Helplessness is embittering.

At this point it must be admitted that we revolutionaries have been defeated. Not because since 2008 we haven't achieved revolution as an objective, but because, under a steady barrage of obscurantism, we've lost sight of of revolution *as a process*. When we fail, we can blame the whole world, making up all sorts of explanations, even scientific ones, based on a thousand resentments, or we can question ourselves about the toeholds which the enemy may have within us that determine the non-accidental, repeated character of our failures. We might inquire, for example, as to what remains of *leftism* among revolutionaries and whether it disposes them not only to defeat but also to a nearly general hostility. A certain way of asserting a moral superiority which they haven't earned is doubtless a quirk inherited from the left. As is the presumed ability to decree the right way to live—the way that is truly progressive, enlightened, modern, correct, deconstructed, and undefiled. A claim to which anyone coming under its summary banishment among the reactionaries-conservatives-obscurantists-narrowminds-bumpkins-fogies will respond with thoughts of murder. Far from creating a distance, the heated rivalry of revolutionaries with the left only keeps us moored to its ground. We should cast off!

Since *The Coming Insurrection*, we've gone to the places where the epoch was inflamed. We've read, we've fought, we've discussed with comrades of every country and every tendency. Together with them, we've come up against the invisible obstacles of the times. Some of us have died, others have seen prison. We've kept going. We haven't given up on constructing worlds or attacking this one. We've returned from our stays abroad with the certainty that we weren't living through erratic, separate revolts that were isolated from each other and would still need to be connected. This is what "news-reporting" constructs and dramatizes in its calculated management of perceptions, being the work of counter-insurrection, which begins at that minute scale. We are not contemporaneous with scattered revolts, but with an unparalleled global wave of uprisings that intercommunicate imperceptibly. Moved by a universal desire to be together that only a universal separation can explain. By a general hatred of the police that expresses a lucid refusal of the general atomization which the police oversees. The same anxiety is visible everywhere, the same deep panic, provoking the same upwellings of dignity, and not indignation. What is happening in the world since 2008 isn't an incoherent series of crazy outbursts occurring suddenly in hermetically sealed countries. It's a single historical sequence unfolding in a strict unity of place and time, from Greece to Chile. And only a *distinctly global* perspective can capture its significance. We can't leave it to the think tanks of capital to spell out the practical implications of this sequence.

However localized it may be, every insurrection gestures beyond itself; it contains something global from the outset. It raises us together to the level of the epoch. But the epoch is also what we find deep within us, that is, when we're willing to descend that far, when we immerse ourselves in what we're experiencing, seeing, feeling, perceiving. There's a way of knowledge in this, and a code of action; there's also what explains the underground connection between the pure intensity of street combat and the unalloyed self-presence of the loner. The epoch must be sought deep within each situation and deep within each person. That is where "we" meet up, where real friends are found, scattered over the globe, but walking the road together.

The conspiracy theorists are counterrevolutionary in one respect at least; they reserve the privilege of conspiracy exclusively for the power elite. While it's obvious that those in power scheme to preserve and extend their positions, it's no less certain that *there's conspiracy everywhere*—in building hallways, at the coffee machine, in the back of kebab houses, at parties, in love affairs, in prisons. Through capillary channels and on a global scale, all these connections, all these conversations, all these friendships are forming a historical party in operation—"our party," as Marx said. Confronting the objective conspiracy of the order of things, there is a diffuse conspiracy of which we are de facto members. But the greatest confusion obtains within it. Everywhere it turns, our party stumbles over its own ideological inheritance. It gets caught up in a whole tangle of defeated and defunct revolutionary traditions, which demand respect nonetheless. But strategic intelligence comes from the heart and not the brain, and the problem with ideology is precisely that it forms a screen between thinking and the heart. To put this differently: we're obliged to force open a door to a space we already occupy. The only party to be built is the one that's already there. We must rid ourselves of all the mental clutter that gets in the way of a clear grasp of our shared situation, our "common terrestritude," to use Gramsci's expression. Our inheritance is not preceded by any will or testament.

Like any advertising slogan, the catchphrase "We are the 99%" owes its effectiveness not to what it says but to what it doesn't say. What it doesn't say is the identity of the *powerful* 1%. What characterizes the 1% is not their wealth—in the United States the wealthy are far more than 1%—it's not their celebrity—they tend to be discreet, and nowadays who doesn't have a right to their fifteen minutes of fame? What characterizes the 1% is that they are *organized*. They even organize in order to organize the lives of others. The truth of this slogan is quite cruel, and it's that the number doesn't matter: one can be 99% and still be completely dominated. Conversely, the collective lootings of Tottenham are a sufficient demonstration that one ceases to be poor as soon as one begins to get organized. There is a considerable difference between a mass of poor people and a mass of poor people determined to act together.

Organizing has never meant affiliation with the same organization. Organizing is acting in accordance with a common perception, at whatever level that may be. Now, what is missing from the situation is not "people's anger" or economic shortage, it's not the good will of militants or the spread of critical consciousness, or even the proliferation of anarchist gestures. What we lack is a shared perception of the situation. Without this binding agent, gestures dissolve without a trace into nothingness, lives have the texture of dreams, and uprisings end up in schoolbooks.

The daily profusion of news, whether alarming or merely scandalous, shapes our conception of a generally unintelligible world. Its chaotic look is the fog of war behind which it is rendered unassailable. Its ungovernable appearance helps to make it governable *in reality*. There is the ruse. By adopting crisis management as a technique of government, capital has not simply replaced the cult of progress with the blackmail of threatened catastrophe; it has arrogated the strategic intelligence of the present, the general assessment of the operations that are under way. This move must be countered. As far as strategy is concerned, it's a matter of getting two steps ahead of global governance. There's not a crisis that we would need to get out of, there's a war that we have to win.

A shared understanding of the situation cannot emerge from one text alone, but requires an international discussion. And for a discussion to take place, statements need to be offered, this being one. We have subjected the revolutionary tradition and positions to the touchstone of the historical situation and sought to cut the thousand ideal threads that keep the Gulliver of revolution attached to the ground. We have groped for the passageways, the gestures, and the thoughts that might allow us to extract ourselves from the impasse of the present. There's no revolutionary movement without a language that can capture the state we find ourselves in as well as the fissure of possibility running through it. What follows is a contribution to its elaboration.

To that end, our text is appearing in eight languages and on four continents at once. If we are everywhere, if we are legion, then we must now organize ourselves, worldwide.

Athens, December 2008.

1

MERRY CRISIS AND HAPPY NEW FEAR

1. Crisis Is a Mode of Government. 2. The Real Catastrophe Is Existential and Metaphysical. 3. The Apocalypse Disappoints.

1. We other revolutionaries are the great cuckolds of modern history. And one is always complicit in some way with one's own betrayal. The fact is painful, so it's generally denied. We've had a blind faith in *crisis*, a faith so blind and so enduring that we didn't see how the liberal order had made it the centerpiece of its arsenal. Marx wrote in the aftermath of 1848: "A new revolution is possible only as a result of a new crisis; but it will come, just as surely as the crisis itself." And indeed he spent the rest of his days prophetizing, with every spasm of the world economy, the great final crisis of capital which he would wait for in vain. There are still Marxists who try to sell us the current crisis as

"The Big One," and would have us wait a bit longer for their curious version of the Last Judgement.

"If you want to force a change," Milton Friedman advised his Chicago Boys, "set off a crisis." Far from fearing crises, capital now tries its hand at producing them experimentally. The way avalanches are intentionally triggered in order to control their timing and size. The way plains are set ablaze so that a menacing fire will extinguish itself there for lack of fuel. "Where and when" is a question of opportuneness or tactical necessity. It's public knowledge that shortly after being appointed, in 2010, the director of the Greek Statistical Authority, ELSTAT, set about falsifying that country's debt accounts, making them look worse as a way of justifying the Troika's intervention. So it's a fact that the "sovereign debt crisis" was launched by a man still on the official payroll of the IMF, an institution charged with "helping" countries get out of debt. Here it was a matter of testing out, in a European country under real conditions, the neoliberal project of a complete revamping of a society, to measure the effects of a proper policy of "structural adjustment."

With its medical connotation, throughout the whole modern period crisis was that natural thing which arose in an unexpected or cyclical way, calling for a decision to be made, a decision that would put an end to the general insecurity of the critical situation. The conclusion would be fortunate or unfortunate depending on the effectiveness of the applied medication. The critical moment was also the moment *of critique*—the brief interval in which discussion concerning the symptoms and the medication was opened. That's no longer the case at present. The remedy is no longer there to put an end to the crisis. On the contrary, the crisis is set off with a view to introducing the remedy. They speak now of "crisis" in regard to what they intend to restructure, just as they label "terrorists" those they are preparing to strike down. The "crisis of the banlieues" in France in 2005 thus served to announce the biggest urban-planning offensive of the last thirty years against the so-called "banlieues," orchestrated directly by the Ministry of the Interior.

The crisis discourse of the neoliberals is a variety of doublespeak. Among themselves they prefer to speak of a "double truth." On one hand, crisis is the invigorating moment of "creative destruction," creating opportunities, innovation, and entrepreneurs of whom only the best, most highly motivated, and most competitive will survive. "Deep down that is probably the message of capitalism: 'creative destruction'—the scrapping of old technologies and old ways of doing things for the new is the only way to raise average living standards [...] Capitalism creates a tug-of-war within each of us. We are alternately the aggressive entrepreneur and the couch potato, who subliminally prefers the lessened competitive stress of an economy where all participants have equal incomes," writes Alan Greenspan, chairman of the American Federal Reserve from 1987 to 2006. On the other hand, the discourse of crisis intervenes as a political method for managing populations. The continuous restructuring of everything—social welfare and organigrams, companies and urban districts—is the only way to ensure the non-existence of the opposing party, through a constant disruption of the conditions of existence. The rhetoric of change is used to dismantle every custom, to break all ties, to unsettle every certainty, to discourage every solidarity, to maintain a chronic existential insecurity. It corresponds to a strategy that can be formulated in these terms: "Use a continuous crisis to avert any actual crisis." On the everyday level, this is akin to the well-known counter-insurgency practice of "destabilizing in order to stabilize," which, for the authorities, consists in deliberately producing chaos so as to make order more desirable than revolution. From micromanagement to the management of whole countries, the population is kept in a kind of constant trauma. The resulting stupefaction and dereliction mean that the managers can do more or less what they want with each and everyone. The mass depression currently afflicting the Greeks is the *deliberate* product of the Troika's policy, and not its collateral effect.

If some commentators made fools of themselves by hastily proclaiming the "death of neoliberalism" with the explosion of the subprime swindle, it's because they failed to understand that the "crisis" was not an economic phenomenon but a political technique of government. We're not experiencing a crisis of capitalism but rather the triumph of crisis capitalism. "Crisis" means: government is growing. Crisis has become the *ultima ratio* of the powers that be. Modernity measured everything in relation to the past backwardness it claimed to be rescuing us from; now everything is measured in relation to its impending collapse. When the salaries of Greek civil servants are reduced by half, it's while pointing out that one could just as well no longer pay them at all. Every time the period of pension contribution of French wage earners is lengthened, the rationale has to do with "saving the retirement system." The present crisis, permanent and omnilateral, is no longer the classic crisis, the decisive moment. On the contrary, it's an endless end, a lasting apocalypse, an indefinite suspension, an effective postponement of the actual collapse, and for that reason a permanent state of exception. The current crisis no longer promises anything; on the contrary, it tends to free whoever governs from every constraint as to the means deployed.

2. Epochs are proud. Each one claims to be unique. Our own prides itself on bringing about the historical collision of a planetary ecological crisis, a generalized crisis of democracies, and an inexorable energy crisis, the whole being crowned by a creeping global economic crisis, but "unmatched for the last hundred years." And this affirms and heightens our pleasure at living through an epoch like no other. But one only has to open the newspapers from the 1970s, or read the Club of Rome report on the *Limits to Growth* from 1972, the article by the cybernetician Gregory Bateson on "The Roots of Ecological Crisis" from March 1970, or *The Crisis of Democracy* published in 1975 by the Trilateral Commission, to see that we've been living under the dark star of integral crisis at least since the begining of the 1970s. A text from 1972 such as Giogio Cesarono's *Apocalypse and Revolution* already analyzes it lucidly. So if the seventh seal was opened at a precise moment, it certainly wasn't yesterday.

At the end of 2012, the highly official American Centers for Disease Control circulated a graphic novel for a change. Its title: *Preparedness 101: Zombie Apocalypse*. The idea is simple: the population must be prepared for any eventuality, a nuclear or natural catastrophe, a general breakdown of the system or an insurrection. The document concludes by saying: "If you're ready for a zombie apocalypse then you're ready for any emergency." The zombie figure comes from Haitian voodoo culture. In American films, masses of rebellious zombies chronically function as an allegory of the threat of a generalized insurrection by the black proletariat. So *that* is clearly what people must be *prepared* for. Now that there's no longer any Soviet threat to wield as a way to ensure the psychotic cohesion of the citizens, anything will do to make sure the population is ready to defend itself—that is, *defend the system*. Maintaining an endless fear to forestall a frightful end.

All of Western false consciousness is compressed into this official comic strip. It's plain to see that the real living dead are the petty bourgeois of the American suburbs. Obvious that the dull concern with survival, the economic worry about not having enough, the feeling of having an unsustainable form of life, is not something that will come after the catastrophe, but what already drives the desperate struggle for life of each individual in a neoliberal regime. Defeated life is not what threatens but what is already there, day after day. Everyone sees it, everyone knows it and feels it. The Walking Dead are the *salary men*. If this epoch is crazy about apocalyptic dramatizations, which make up a large share of film production, there's more involved than the aesthetic enjoyment which the distraction authorizes. Besides, John's *Revelation* already has a whole Hollywood-style phantasmagoria with its air attacks by furious angels, its horrendous floods, its spectacular scourges. Only universal destruction, the death of everything, comes close to giving the suburban employee the feeling he's alive, since he's the *least alive* of all the creatures. "To hell with it all" and "let's pray that it lasts" are the two sighs heaved alternately by the same civilized distress. An old Calvinist taste for mortification has a part in this: life is a reprieve, never a plenitude. The discussions of "European nihilism" were not vain talk. Indeed, nihilism is an article that's been exported so successfully that the world is now saturated with it. As regards "neoliberal globalization," one could say that what we now have above all is the globalization of nihilism.

In 2007 we wrote that "what we are faced with is not the crisis of a society but the extinction of a civilization." At the time, this kind of statement got you taken for an Illuminatus. But "the crisis" has gone down that path. And even ATTAC acknowledges a "crisis of civilization"—which goes to show. More dramatically, an American veteran of the Iraq war turned "strategy" consultant, wrote in the autumn of 2013 in the *New York Times*: "Now, when I look into our future, I see water rising up to wash out lower Manhattan. I see food riots, hurricanes, and climate refugees. I see 82nd Airborne soldiers shooting looters. I see grid failure, wrecked harbors, Fukushima waste, and plagues. I see Baghdad. I see the Rockaways underwater. I see a strange, precarious world […] The biggest problem climate change poses isn't how the Department of Defense should plan for resource wars, or how we should put up sea walls to protect Alphabet City, or when we should evacuate Hoboken. It won't be addressed by buying a Prius, signing a treaty, or turning off the air-conditioning. The biggest problem we face is a philosophical one: understanding that this civilization is *already dead*." In the days after the First World War it still only called itself "mortal," which it certainly was, in every sense of the word.

In reality, the end of civilization has been clinically established for a century, and countersigned by events. Expatiating on the matter is now nothing but a means of distraction. But it's a distraction from the catastrophe *there in front of us*, and that has been there for a long time, from the catastrophe that *we are*, the catastrophe that *the West is*. That catastrophe is existential, affective, and metaphysical first of all. It resides in Western man's incredible estrangement from the world, an estrangement that demands, for example, that he become the master and possessor of nature—one only seeks to possess what one fears. It's not for nothing that he has placed so many *screens* between himself and the world. By cutting himself off from what exists, Western man has made it into this desolate expanse, this dreary, hostile, mechanical, absurd nothingness which he must ceaselessly devastate, through his *labor*, his cancerous activism, his shallow hysterical agitation. Relentlessly driven from euphoria to stupor and from stupor to euphoria, he tries to remedy his absence from the world through a whole accumulation of expertise, prostheses, and relations, a whole technological hardware store that is ultimately disappointing. He's more and more visibly that *overequipped existentialist* who can't stop engineering everything, recreating everything, unable as he is to bear a reality that is completely beyond him. As that moron, Camus, blandly admitted, "For a man, understanding the world means reducing it to the human, stamping it with his seal." He tries humbly to re-enchant his divorce from existence, from himself, from "other people"—that hell!—by calling it his "freedom," when it's not by resorting to dismal parties, stupid entertainments, or heavy drug use. Life is effectively, affectively, absent for him, because life repels him. Deep down, it *nauseates* him. He's managed to protect himself from everything reality contains that is unstable, irreducible, palpable, corporal, weighty, hot, or fatiguing by projecting it onto the ideal, visual, distant, and digitized plane of the Internet, where there's no friction or tears, no death or odors.

The falsity of the entire Western apocalyptic consists in projecting onto the world the mourning we're not able to do in regard to it. It's not the world that is lost, it's *we* who have lost the world and go on losing it. It's not the world that is going to end *soon*, it's *we* who *are finished*, amputated, cut-off, *we* who refuse vital contact with the real in a hallucinatory way. The crisis is not economic, ecological, or political, *the crisis is above all that of presence*. To such a point that the *must* of commodities—the iPhone and the Hummer being exemplary cases—consists in a sophisticated absence outfit. On the one hand, the iPhone concentrates all the possible accesses to the world and to others in a single object. It is the lamp and the camera, the mason's level and the musician's recording device, the TV and the compass, the tourist guide and the means of communication; on the other, it is the prosthesis that bars any openness to what is there and places me in a regime of constant, convenient semi-presence, retaining a part of my being-there in its grip. They've even launched a smartphone app designed to remedy the fact that "our 24/7 connection to the digital world disconnects us from the real world around us." It is brightly called the *GPS for the Soul*. As for the Hummer, it's the possibility of transporting my autistic bubble, my impermeability to everything, into the most inaccessible recesses of "nature" and coming back *intact*. That Google has declared the "fight against death" to be a new industrial horizon shows how one can be mistaken *about what life is*.

At the apex of his insanity, Man has even proclaimed himself a "geological force," going so far as to give the name of his species to a phase of the life of the planet: he's taken to speaking of an "anthropocene." For the last time, he assigns himself the main role, even if it's to accuse himself of having trashed everything—the seas and the skies, the ground and what's underground—even if it's to confess his guilt for the unprecedented extinction of plant and animal species. But what's remarkable is that he continues relating in the same disastrous manner to the disaster produced by his own disastrous relationship with the world. He *calculates* the rate at which the ice pack is disappearing. He *measures* the extermination of the non-human forms of life. As to climate change, he doesn't talk about it based on his sensible experience—a bird that doesn't return in the same period of the year, an insect whose sounds aren't heard anymore, a plant that no longer flowers at the same time as some other one. He talks about it scientifically with numbers and averages. He thinks he's saying something when he establishes that the temperature will rise so many degrees and the precipitation will decrease by so many inches or millimeters. He even speaks of "biodiversity." He observes the rarefaction of life on earth *from space*. He has the hubris to claim, paternally, to be "protecting the environment," which certainly never asked for anything of the sort. All this has the look of a last bold move in a game that can't be won.

The objective disaster serves mainly to mask another disaster, this one more obvious still and more massive. The exhaustion of natural resources is probably less advanced than the exhaustion of subjective resources, of vital resources, that is afflicting our contemporaries. If so much satisfaction is derived from surveying the devastation of the environment it's largely because this veils the shocking destruction of interiorities. Every oil spill, every sterile plain, every species extinction is an image of our souls in shreds, a reflection of our absence from the world, of our personal inability to inhabit it. Fukushima offers the spectacle of this complete failure of man and his mastery, which only produces ruins—and those Japanese plains, intact in appearance but where no one can live for decades. A never-ending decomposition that is finishing the job of making the world uninhabitable: the West will have ended up borrowing its mode of existence from what it fears the most— radioactive waste.

When one asks the left of the left what the revolution would consist in, it is quick to answer: "placing the human at the center." What that left doesn't realize is how tired of the human the world is, how tired of humanity we are—of that species that thought it was the jewel of creation, that believed it was entitled to ravage everything since everything belonged to it. "Placing the human at the center" was the Western project. We know how that turned out. The time has come to jump ship, to betray the species. There's no great human family that would exist separately from each of its worlds, from each of its familiar universes, each of the forms of life that are strewn across the earth. There is no humanity, there are only earthlings and their enemies, the Occidentals, of whatever skin color they happen to be. We other revolutionaries, with our atavistic humanism, would do well to inform ourselves about the uninterrupted uprisings by the indigenous peoples of Central and South America over the past twenty years. Their watchword could be "Place the earth at the center." It's a declaration of war *against Man*. Declaring war on him could be the best way to bring him back down to earth, if only he didn't play deaf, as always.

3. On December 21, 2012, no fewer than 300 journalists from 18 countries invaded the little village of Bugarach in the Aude *département* of

France. No end of time was ever announced for that date on any Mayan calendar deciphered so far. The rumor that this village had some slight connection with that non-existent prophecy was an obvious practical joke. The television broadcasters dispatched a swarm of reporters to the place nonetheless. One was curious to see if there *really are* people who believe in the end of the world, since we can't even manage to believe in that any more, and have the hardest time believing in our own loves. At Bugarach on that day, there was no one, no one apart from the numerous celebrants of the spectacle. The reporters were reduced to talking about themselves, about their pointless wait, their boredom and the fact that nothing was happening. Caught in their own trap, they revealed the true face of the end-of-the-world: journalists, waiting, and events that refuse to happen.

One shouldn't underestimate the craving for apocalypse, the lust for Armageddon that permeates the epoch. Its particular existential pornography involves ogling prefigurative documentaries showing clouds of computer-animated grasshoppers descending on the Bordeaux vineyards in 2075, juxtaposed with "climate migrants" storming the southern shores of Europe—the same migrants that Frontex is already making a point of decimating. Nothing is older than the end of the world. The apocalyptic passion has always been favored by the powerless since earliest antiquity. What is new in our epoch is that the apocalyptic has been totally absorbed by capital, and placed in its service. The horizon of catastrophe is what we are currently being governed by. Now, if there is one thing destined to remain unfulfilled, it's the apocalyptic prophecy, be it economic, climatic, terrorist, or nuclear. It is pronounced only in order to summon the means of averting it, which is to say, most often, the necessity of government. No organization, whether political or religious, has ever declared itself defeated because the facts contradicted its prophecies. Because the purpose of prophecy is never to be right about the future, but to *act upon the present*: to impose a waiting mode, passivity, submission, here and now.

Not only is there no catastrophe to come other than the one that's already here, it's evident that most actual disasters offer an escape from our daily disaster. Many examples attest to the relief from existential apocalypse that real disaster brings, from the earthquake that struck San Francisco in 1906 to Hurricane Sandy that devastated New York in 2012. One generally assumes that the relations between people in an emergency situation reveal their deep and eternal bestiality. With every destructive earthquake, every economic crash and every "terrorist attack," one *desires* to see a confirmation of the old chimera of the state of nature and its train of uncontrollable violent acts. When the thin dikes of civilization give way, one would like for the "vile core of man" that obsessed Pascal to show itself, that "human nature" with its evil passions—envious, brutal, blind and despicable—which has served the holders of power as an argument at least since Thucydides. Unfortunately the fantasy has been disconfirmed by most of the historically known disasters.

The disappearance of a civilization generally doesn't take the form of a chaotic war of all against all. In a situation of extreme catastrophe, that hostile discourse only serves to justify the priority given to the defense of property against looting, by the police, the army or, for lack of anything better, by *vigilante* militias formed for the occasion. It can also serve to cover misappropriations by the authorities themselves, like those of the Italian Civil Protection Department after the Aquila earthquake. On the contrary, the decomposition of this world, taken on as such, creates openings for other ways of living, including in the middle of an "emergency situation." Consider the inhabitants of Mexico City in 1985, who, among the ruins of their neighborhoods struck by a deadly quake, reinvented the revolutionary carnival and the figure of the superhero serving the people—in the form of a legendary wrestler, Super Barrio. In the euphoria of regaining control of their urban existence, they conflated the collapse of buildings with a break-down of the political system, releasing the life of the city from the grip of government as much as possible and starting to rebuild their destroyed dwellings. An enthusiastic resident of Halifax said something similar when he declared after the hurricane of 2003: "Everybody woke up the next morning and everything was different. There was no electricity, all the stores were closed, no one had access to media. The consequence was that everyone poured out into the street to bear witness. Not quite a street party, but everyone out at once—it was a happy feeling to see everybody even though we didn't know each other." The same as with those miniature communities formed spontaneously in New Orleans in the days after Katrina, faced with the contempt of the public authorities and the paranoia of the security agencies, communities that organized daily to feed and clothe themselves and attend to each other's needs, even if this required looting a store or two.

To start with, therefore, rethinking an idea of revolution capable of interrupting the disastrous course of things is to purge it of every apocalyptic element it has contained up to now. It is to see that Marxist eschatology differs *only in that regard* from the imperial founding aspiration of the United States—the one still printed on every dollar bill: "*Annuit coeptis. Novus ordo seclorum.*" Socialists, liberals, Saint-Simonians, and Cold War Russians and Americans have always expressed the same neurasthenic yearning for the establishment of an era of peace and sterile abundance where there would no longer be anything to fear, where the contradictions would finally be resolved and the negative would be tamed. The dream of a prosperous society, established through science and industry, one that was totally automated and finally pacified. Something like an earthly paradise organized on the model of a psychiatric hospital or a sanitorium. An ideal that can only come from seriously ill beings who no longer even hope for a remission. "Heaven is a place where nothing ever happens," the song says.

The whole originality and the whole scandal of Marxism was to claim that to reach the millennium it was necessary to pass through the economic apocalypse, whereas the others judged the latter to be superfluous. We won't wait for the millennium or the apocalypse. There will never be peace on earth. Abandoning the idea of peace is the only real peace. Faced with the Western catastrophe, the left generally adopts the position of lamentation, denunciation, and thus helplessness, which makes it loathsome in the eyes of the very ones it claims to be defending. The state of exception in which we are living shouldn't be denounced, it should be turned back against power itself. We will then be relieved in our turn of any consideration for the law—in proportion to the impunity that we claim, and depending on the relative force that we create. We have an absolutely clear field for any decision, any initiative, as long as they're linked to a careful reading of the situation. For us there is now only a historical battlefield, and the forces that move upon it. Our range of action is boundless. Historical life extends her arms to us. There are countless reasons to refuse her, but they all spring from neurosis. Confronted with the apocalypse in a recent zombie film, a former United Nations official comes to this clearheaded conclusion: "It's not the end, not even close. If you can fight, fight. Help each other. The war has just begun."

2

THEY WANT TO OBLIGE US TO GOVERN. WE WON'T YIELD TO THAT PRESSURE.

1. Characteristic Features of Contemporary Insurrections. 2. There's No Such Thing as a Democratic Insurrection. 3. Democracy Is Just Government in Its Pure State. 4. Theory of Destitution.

1. A man dies. He was killed by the police, directly, indirectly. He's anyone, an unemployed person, a "dealer" of something or other, a high school student, in London, Sidi Bouzid, Athens, or Clichy-sous-Bois. He's said to be a "young person," whether he's 16 or 30. He's called a "young person" because he's socially nil, and because, back when one became someone on reaching adulthood, the young people were precisely those who were still nobodies.

A man dies, a country rises up. The one is not the cause of the other, just the detonator. Alexandros Grigoropoulos, Mark Duggan, Mohamed Bouazizi,

Oaxaca, 2006.

Massinissa Guesma—the name of a dead person became, during those days, those weeks, the proper name of the general anonymity, of the shared dispossession. And at its beginning, insurrection is the doing of those who are nothing, of those who hang out in the cafés, in the streets, in life, at the university, on the Internet. It coalesces the whole floating element, plebeian and petty bourgeois, that is secreted in excess by the continuous disintegration of the social. Everything regarded as marginal, obsolete, or without prospects returns to the center. At Sidi Bouzid, Kasserine, Thala, it was the "crazies," the "lost souls," the "good-for-nothings," the "freaks" who first spread the news of the death of their companion in misery. They climbed onto chairs, tables, monuments, in all the public places all over town. Their tirades stirred everyone willing to listen. Right behind them, there were the high school students who swung into action, those without any remaining hope of a career.

The uprising lasts a few days or a few months, and brings about the fall of the regime or the exposing of every illusion of social peace. It is itself anonymous: no leader, no organization, no demands, no program. The slogans, when there are any, seem to reach no farther than the negation of the existing order, and they are abrupt: "Clear out!," "The people want the system to fall!," "We don't care about your shit." "Tayyip, winter is coming." On TV, on the airwaves, the authorities pound out their same old rhetoric: "they're gangs of *çapulcu* [looters], smashers, terrorists out of nowhere, most likely in the pay of foreign interests." Those who've risen up have no one to put on the throne as a replacement, perhaps just a question mark instead. It's not the bottom dogs, or the working class, or the petty bourgeoisie, or the multitudes who are rebelling. They don't form anything homogenous enough to have a representative. There's no new revolutionary subject whose emergence had eluded observers. So if it's said that the "people" are in the streets it's not a people that existed previously, but rather the people that previously *were lacking*. It's not the people that produce an uprising, it's the uprising that produces its people, by re-engendering the shared experience and understanding, the human fabric and the real-life language that had disappeared. Revolutions of the past promised a new life. Contemporary insurrections deliver the keys to it. The shifts made by the Cairo ultras were not those of groups who were revolutionary before the "revolution." Before, they were only gangs capable of organizing against the police. It's from having played such an important role during the "revolution" that they were forced by the situation to raise questions usually reserved for "revolutionaries." There is where the *event* resides: not in the media phenomenon fabricated to exploit the rebellion through external celebration of it, but in the encounters actually produced within it. This is something much less spectacular than "the movement" or "the revolution," but more decisive. No one can say what an encounter is capable of generating.

This is how insurrections continue, in a molecular fashion, imperceptibly, in the life of neighborhoods, collectives, squats, "social centers," and singular beings, in Brazil as in Spain, in Chile as in Greece. Not because they implement a political program but because they trigger revolutionary becomings. Because what was lived through shines with such a glow that those who had the experience have to be faithful to it, not separating off but constructing what *was missing from their lives before.* If the Spanish movement of plaza occupations, once it had disappeared from the media radar screen, had not been continued in the neighborhoods of Barcelona and elsewhere via a process of communalization and self-organization, the attempt to destroy the Can Vies squat in June of 2014 would not have been placed in check by three days of rioting by the whole Sants district and we would not have seen a whole city participating in rebuilding the site that was attacked. There would have been just a few squatters protesting against another eviction in a climate of indifference. The construction in question here is not that of a "new society" at its embryonic stage, nor an organization that will eventually overthrow an authority so as to constitute a new one, it's the collective power which, with its consistency and its intelligence, consigns the ruling power to powerlessness, foiling each of its maneuvers in turn.

Very often the revolutionaries are those whom the revolutions take by surprise. But in contemporary insurrections there is something that especially unsettles the revolutionaries: the insurrections no longer base themselves on political ideologies, but on *ethical truths*. Here we have two words that, to a modern sensibility, sound like an oxymoron when they're brought together. Establishing what is true is the role of science, is it not?—science having nothing to do with moral norms and other contingent values. For moderns, there is the World on one side, themselves on the other, and language to bridge the gulf. A truth, we were taught, is a solid point above the abyss—a statement that adequately *describes* the World. We've conveniently forgotten the slow apprenticeship during which we acquired, together with language, a relationship with the world. Far from serving to describe the world, language helps us rather to *construct* a world. Ethical truths are thus not truths *about* the world, but truths on the basis of which we dwell therein. These are truths, affirmations, stated or not, that are felt but not proved. The silent gaze, fists closed, into the eyes of the little boss, staring him down for a long minute, is one such truth, and worth as much as the loud phrase, "one is always right to rebel." Truths are what *bind* us, to ourselves, to the world around us, and to each other. They give us entry into an immediately shared life, an undetached existence, regardless of the illusory walls of our Selves. If earthlings are prepared to risk their lives to prevent a square from being transformed into a parking lot as at Gamonal in Spain, a park from becoming a shopping center as at Gezi in Turkey, woods from becoming an airport as at Notre-Dame-des-Landes, it's clearly because what we love, what we are attached to—beings, places, or ideas—is also part of us, because we are not reducible to a Self lodging for a lifetime in a physical body bounded by its skin, the whole entity being graced with a set of *properties* which this Self believes it possesses. When the world is fucked with, it's we ourselves who are being attacked.

Paradoxically, even where an ethical truth is uttered as a refusal, the fact of saying "No!" places us squarely in existence. Just as paradoxically, the individual is discovered to be so unindividual that sometimes the suicide of a single one can collapse the whole edifice of social untruth. Mohamed Bouazizi's gesture involving self-immolation in front of the Sidi Bouzid prefecture is sufficient evidence of this. Its explosive power is due to the potent affirmation it contains. It says, "The life laid out for us is not worth living," "We weren't born to let ourselves be humiliated like that by the police," "You can reduce us to nothing, but you'll never take away the share of sovereignty that belongs to living beings," or "Look at us little people, barely existing, humiliated, see how we're beyond the miserable means by which you cling to your sick man's power." That is what was distinctly heard in the gesture. If the televised interview, in Egypt, of Wael Ghonim after his secret incarceration by the "services" had the effect of reversing the situation, it's because a truth broke through his tears and also exploded in the hearts of everyone. In the same vein, during the first weeks of Occupy Wall Street, before the usual movement managers instituted their little "working groups" responsible for preparing the decisions which the assembly would only need to approve, the model for the speeches made to the 1500 persons present was the guy who stepped forward one day and said, "Yo! What up? My name is Mike. I'm just a gangster from Harlem. I hate my life. Fuck my boss! Fuck my girlfriend! Fuck the cops! Just wanted to say, I'm happy to be here, with you all." And his words were repeated seven times by the chorus of "human megaphones" that had replaced the microphones prohibited by the police.

The true content of Occupy Wall Street was not the demand, tacked onto the movement a posteriori like a post-it stuck on a hippopotamus, for better wages, decent housing, or a more generous social security, but *disgust with the life we're forced to live*. Disgust with a life in which we're all *alone*, alone facing the necessity for each one to make a living, house oneself, feed oneself, realize one's potential, and attend to one's health, *by oneself*. Disgust with the miserable form of life of the metropolitan individual—scrupulous distrust/ refined, *smart* skepticism/shallow, ephemeral loves/resulting extreme sexualization of every encounter/then the periodic return to a comfortable and desperate separation/constant distraction, hence ignorance of oneself, hence fear of oneself, hence fear of the other. The life in common that was attempted in Zuccotti Park, in tents, in the cold, in the rain, surrounded by police in the dreariest of Manhattan's squares, was definitely not a full rollout of the *vita nova*—it was just the point where the sadness of metropolitan existence began to be flagrant. At last it was possible to grasp our shared condition *together*, our equal reduction to the status of entrepreneurs of the self. That existential epiphany was the pulsing heart of Occupy Wall Street, for as long as it was fresh and lively.

What is at issue in contemporary insurrections is knowing what a desirable form of life would be, and not the nature of the institutions that would loom over it. But recognizing this would immediately mean recognizing the ethical inanity of the West. And this would rule out attributing the victory of this or that Islamic party after this or that uprising to a presumed mental backwardness of the populations. It would have to be admitted on the contrary that the strength of the Islamists lies precisely in the fact that their political ideology presents itself as a system of ethical prescriptions first of all. To put it differently, if they were more successful than the other politicians, it's precisely because they didn't situate themselves mainly on the terrain of politics. And so people here in France can stop whining or crying wolf every time an earnest adolescent chooses to join the ranks of the "jihadists" instead of our suicidal army of wage workers of the service sector. And, adults that we are, it may be possible for us to accept the face we discover in that unflattering mirror.

In Slovenia in 2012, in the calm city of Maribor, a street revolt erupted which inflamed a good part of the country in the days that followed. Such a thing was unexpected in a country with Swisslike features. But what is more surprising is that its starting point was the revelation that road-radar flashes were proliferating in the city because a private company was pocketing nearly all the fines. Could anything be less "political" as the starting point of an insurrection than radar flashes? But could anything be more ethical than the refusal to let oneself be fleeced like sheep? It's like a 21st century Michael Kohlhaas. The importance of the theme of prevailing corruption in almost all the contemporary revolts shows that they are ethical before being political, or that they are political precisely to the degree that they're contemptuous of politics, including radical politics. As long as being of the left will mean denying the existence of ethical truths and correcting for that impairment with a morality that's as feeble as it is expedient, the fascists will continue to look like the only affirmative political force, being the only ones who don't apologize for living as they do. They'll go from success to success, and will go on deflecting the energy of nascent revolts back against themselves.

This may also be the reason for the failure, incomprehensible otherwise, of all the "anti-austerity movements" which, given current conditions, should take off like wildfire, but instead are sluggishly relaunching in Europe for the tenth time. The problem is that the question of austerity is not being addressed on the ground where it's truly situated: that of a serious disagreement about what it means to live, to live *well*. Put in a summary way, austerity in countries with a Protestant culture tends to be seen as a virtue, whereas in a large part of southern Europe being austere basically means being a pathetic loser. What is happening currently is not just that some are trying to impose an economic austerity on others who don't want to accept it. It's that some consider austerity to be a good thing in the absolute, while others consider it to be, without really daring to say so, an absolute misery. Limiting oneself to fighting against austerity doesn't just add to the misunderstanding, it also ensures that one will lose, by implicitly accepting an idea of life that one doesn't agree with. We don't have to look elsewhere for an explanation of "people's" reluctance to throw themselves into a battle that is already lost. What is required rather is to acknowledge what the conflict is really about: a certain Protestant idea of happiness—being hardworking, thrifty, sober, honest, diligent, temperate, modest, reserved—is being pushed everywhere in Europe. What is needed for contesting the austerity plans is a *different idea of life*, which consists for example in sharing rather than economizing, conversing rather than not saying a word, fighting rather than suffering, celebrating our victories rather than disallowing them, engaging rather than keeping one's distance. Something should be said in this connection about the incalculable strength given to the indigenous movements of the American subcontinent by their embrace of *buen vivir* as a *political* affirmation. On one hand, it brings out the visible contours of what one is fighting for and what against; on the other, it opens one up to a calm discovery of the thousand other ways the "good life" can be understood, ways that are not enemy ways for being different, at least not necessarily.

2. Western rhetoric is unsurprising. Every time a mass uprising takes down a satrap still honored in all the embassies only yesterday, it's because the people "aspire to democracy." The stratagem is as old as Athens. And it works so well that even an Occupy Wall Street assembly saw fit, in November 2011, to allocate 29,000 dollars to twenty or so international observers to go monitor the Egyptian elections. Which drew this response from comrades of Tahrir Square, who were intended recipients of the assistance: "In Egypt, we didn't make the revolution in the street just for the purpose of having a parliament. Our struggle—which we hope to share with you—is broader in scope than the acquisition of a well-oiled parliamentary democracy."

That one is fighting *against* a tyrant doesn't mean that one is fighting *for* democracy—one may also be fighting for a different tyrant, for the caliphate, or for the simple joy of fighting. But above all, if there is one thing that has nothing to do with any arithmetical principle of majority, it is insurrections, the victory of which depends on qualitative criteria—having to do with determination, courage, self-confidence, strategic sense, collective energy. If for two whole centuries elections have been the most widely used instrument after the army for suppressing insurrections, it's clearly because the insurgents are never a majority. As for the pacifism that is associated so naturally with the idea of democracy, we should hear what the Cairo comrades say about that as well: "Those who say that the Egyptian revolution was peaceful did not see the horrors that the police visited upon us, nor did they see the resistance and even the force that revolutionaries used against the police to defend their tentative occupations and spaces: by the government's own admission, 99 police stations were put to the torch, thousands of police cars were destroyed and all of the ruling party's offices around Egypt were burned down." Insurrection doesn't respect any of the formalisms, any of the democratic procedures. Like any large-scale demonstration, it imposes its own ways of using public space. Like any specific strike, it is a politics of the accomplished fact. It is the reign of initiative, of practical complicity, of gesture. As to decision, it accomplishes that in the streets, reminding those who've forgotten, that "popular" comes from the Latin *populor*, "to ravage, devastate." It is a fullness of expression—in the chants, on the walls, in the spoken interventions, in the street—and a nullity of deliberation. Perhaps the miracle of insurrection can be summed up in this way: at the same time that it dissolves democracy as a problem, it speaks immediately of a beyond-democracy.

As we know, there's no shortage of ideologists, such as Antonio Negri and Michael Hardt, who will deduce from the uprisings of the past few years that "the constitution of a democratic society is on the agenda" and propose to make us "capable of democracy" by teaching us the "skills, talents, and knowledges necessary for governing ourselves." For them, as a Spanish Negriist encapsulates it none too neatly: "From Tahrir to the Puerta del Sol, from Syntagma Square to Plaça Catalunya, a cry is repeated from plaza to plaza: 'Democracy!' That is the name of the specter that is moving through the world today." And in fact everything would be all right if the democratic rhetoric were nothing more than a voice emanating from heaven and applied to every uprising from the exterior, either by those governing or by those wanting to succeed them. People would receive it piously, like a priest's homily, while trying not to laugh. But one has to admit that this rhetoric has an actual hold on minds, on hearts, on struggles, as the much talked about "indignants" movement attests. We write "indignants" between quotes because in the first week of the Puerta del Sol occupation, reference was made to Tahrir Square, but no mention of the innocuous little volume by the Socialist Stéphane Hessel, which advocates a citizens' insurrection of "consciences" only as a way of averting the threat of a real insurrection. It was only after a recoding operation conducted in the second week of occupation by the newspaper *El País*, also linked to the Socialist Party, that the movement received its peevish name, which is to say, a good part of its echo and the signifier of its limits. Something related happened in Greece, moreover, where the occupiers of Syntagma Square rejected the label "aganaktismenoi" ("indignants") which the media had stuck on them, opting en bloc to call themselves the "movement of the squares." All in all, with its factual neutrality "movement of the squares" accounts for the complexity, indeed the confusion, of those strange assemblies where Marxists cohabited with Buddhists of the Tibetan way, and Syriza adherents with bourgeois patriots. Spectacle's maneuver is well known, which consists in taking symbolic control of movements by celebrating them in a first phase *for what they are not*, the better to bury them when the right moment comes. By assigning indignation as their content, one was consigning them to helplessness and untruth. "No one lies more than the indignant man," Nietzsche observed. He lies about his estrangement from what makes him indignant, pretending he has no part in what upsets him. He postulates his powerlessness so as to wash his hands of any responsibility for the way things are going; then he converts it into a *moral* affect, into an affect of moral *superiority*. He *believes he has rights*, poor thing. While angry crowds have been known to make revolutions, indignant masses have never been known to do anything but protest powerlessly. The bourgeoisie takes offense, then takes revenge; the petty bourgeoisie waxes indignant, then goes back to the doghouse.

The slogan that was associated with the "movement of the squares" was that of "Democracia real ya!" because the occupation of the Puerta del Sol was initiated by about fifteen "hacktivists" at the conclusion of a demonstration called by the platform with that name on the 15th of May, 2011— "15M" as they say there. Here it was not a question of direct democracy as in the workers' councils, of even true democracy in the style of antiquity, but *real* democracy. It's not surprising that the "movement of the squares" was established, in Athens, a stone's throw from the place of *formal* democracy, the National Assembly. Up to then we had naively thought that real democracy was the kind that was there, as we'd known it forever, with its electoral promises made to be broken, its recording chambers called "parliaments," and its pragmatic negotiations aimed at fooling the world for the benefit of the different lobbies. But for the "hacktivists" of 15M, democracy's reality was the betrayal of "real democracy." That it was cybermilitants who launched the movement is not insignificant. The slogan "real democracy" means this: technologically, your elections that take place once every five years, your pudgy representatives who don't know how to use a computer, your assemblies that resemble a bad theater play or a free-for-all—all this is obsolete. In today's world, thanks to the new communication technologies, thanks to the Internet, biometric identification, smartphones, social networks, you are completely outmoded. It is possible to set up a real democracy, that is a continuous polling, in real time, of the opinion of the population, to really submit every decision to them before making it. An author anticipated this in the 1920s: "One can imagine that one day some subtle inventions will permit everyone to express their opinions about political problems at any time without leaving their homes, thanks to equipment that would record all these opinions on a central device where we could simply read the results." For him this would be "a proof of the absolute privatization of the State and of public life." And, though they were gathered on one plaza, it was this constant polling that the raised and lowered hands of the "indignants" would silently manifest during the successive speeches. Here even the old power to acclaim or jeer had been taken away from the crowd.

On one hand, the movement of the squares was the projection—the crash—of the cybernetic fantasy of universal citizenship onto reality, and on the other an exceptional time of encounters, actions, celebrations, and reappropriations of communal life. This is what eluded the eternal microbureaucracy that tries to pass off its ideological whims for "assembly positions" and seeks to control everything based on the requirement that every action, every gesture, every declaration be "validated by the assembly" to have the right to exist. For all the others, this movement had laid to rest the myth of the general assembly, that is, the myth of its central role. The first evening, May 16, 2011, at the Plaça Catalunya in Barcelona there were 100 persons, the next day 1000, 10,000 the day after, and the first two weekends there were 30,000 persons. So everyone could observe that when so many were present there was no longer any difference between direct democracy and representative democracy. The assembly is where one is forced to listen to bullshit without being able to reply, just like in front of the TV, in addition to being the place of an exhausting theatricality all the more false for its mimicking of sincerity, affliction, or enthusiasm. The extreme bureaucratization of committees got the better of the toughest participants, and apparently it took two weeks for the "content" committee to deliver up an unbearable and calamitous document that, in its opinion, summed up "what we believe in." To a point that, seeing the ridiculousness of the situation, some anarchists put to the vote that the assembly become simply a space for discussion and an information nexus, and not a decision-making body. The thing was comical: voting on not voting anymore. More comical still: the voting was sabotaged by thirty or so Trotskyists. And since that type of micropoliticians exudes boredom and hunger for power in equal measure, everyone ended up avoiding the tiresome assemblies. No surprise, many Occupy participants had the same experience, and drew the same conclusion from it. In Oakland and Chapel Hill alike, people concluded that the assembly had no business validating what any group could do or intended to do, that it was a place of exchange and not of decision. When an idea voiced in an assembly *took*, it was simply that there were enough people who thought it was good enough to be implemented, and not owing to a principle of majority. The decisions took, materialized, or didn't; they were never made. In this way Syntagma Square voted "in general assembly," one June day, 2011, with several thousand *individuals* voting, to initiate actions in the subway; on the scheduled day, however, not twenty persons showed up at the rendezvous prepared to act in an effective way. Thus the problem of "decision-making," an obsession of all the flipped-out democrats of the world, is revealed to have been nothing but a false problem from the beginning.

The fact that, with the movement of the squares, the *fetishism* of the general assembly fell into the void doesn't tarnish the assembly *practice* in the least. We just have to keep in mind that nothing different can come out of an assembly than what is there already. If, on the same plaza, thousands of strangers are brought together, who don't share anything apart from the fact of being there, we can't expect that anything more will emerge from it than what their separation authorizes. One shouldn't imagine for example that an assembly will somehow by itself create the mutual trust necessary for risking an illegal action together. That something so repugnant as an assembly of co-proprietors is possible should already put us on our guard against the passion for GA's. What an assembly actualizes is simply the degree of existing commonality. An assembly of students is not a neighborhood assembly, which is not a neighbor-hood assembly organizing against the neighborhood's "restructuring." An assembly of workers is not the same at the beginning of a strike and at the end of one. And it definitely bears little resemblance to a popular assembly of Oaxacan peoples. The only thing an assembly can produce, with the right effort, is a shared language. Where the only experience in common is separation, one will only hear the amorphous language of separated life. Then indignation is in fact the maximum political intensity attainable by the atomized individual, who mistakes his screen for the world just as he mistakes his feelings for his thoughts. A plenary assembly of all these atoms, in spite of its touching togetherness, will only expose the paralysis induced by a false understanding of the political, and hence their inability to alter the world's drift in the slightest. It makes one think of a sea of dumbstruck faces pressed against a glass wall and watching the mechanical universe continuing to function without them. The feeling of collective helplessness, after the joy of meeting up and *being counted*, did as much to scatter the owners of those "Quechua" tents as the clubs and the tear gas attacks did.

Yet it's true that there was something going beyond that feeling in these occupations, and it was precisely those things that had no place in the theatrical moment of the assembly, everything having to do with the miraculous ability of living beings to *inhabit*, to inhabit even the uninhabitable: the heart of the metropolis. In the occupied squares, all that politics since classical Greece has basically held in contempt, and relegated to the sphere of "economy," of domestic management, "survival," "reproduction," "daily routine," and "labor," was affirmed instead as a dimension of collective political potential, escaping in this way from the subordination of the private. The organizational ability that was routinely demonstrated every day and that managed to feed 3,000 persons at every meal, construct a village in a few days, or take care of wounded rioters can be seen as marking the real political victory of the "movement of the squares." To which the occupation of Taksim and Maidan added the art of maintaining barricades and making Molotov cocktails in industrial quantities.

The fact that a form of organization as banal and predictable as the assembly was invested with such an intense veneration says a lot about the nature of democratic *affects*. If insurrection has to do with anger at first, then with joy, direct democracy, with its formalism, is an affair of worriers. We want to be sure that nothing will occur that is not covered by some procedure. That no event will exceed our capacities. That the situation will remain something we can handle. That no one will feel cheated or in open conflict with the majority. That absolutely no one will ever have to count on their own powers to make themselves understood. That no one will impose anything on anyone. To that end, the different mechanisms of the assembly—from turn-taking to silent applause—organize a cottony space with no edges other than those of a succession of monologues, disabling the need to fight for what one thinks. If democrats must structure the situation to this degree, it's because they have no trust in it. And if they don't trust the situation, this is because at bottom they *don't trust themselves.* Their fear of allowing themselves to be overwhelmed by the situation makes them want to control democracy at any cost, even if this often means destroying it. Democracy is first of all the set of procedures by which it gives form and structure to this anxiety. It doesn't make much sense to denounce democracy: one doesn't denounce an anxiety.

We can only be freed from our attachment to democratic procedures through a general deploying of attention—attention not only to what is being said, but mostly to what is unspoken, attention to the way things are said, and to what can be read on people's faces and in silences. It's a matter of swamping the emptiness that democracy maintains between the individual atoms by a full attention to one another, a new attention to the world we have in common. What's called for is to replace the mechanical regime of argumentation with a regime of truth, of openness, of sensitivity to what is there. In the 12th century, when Tristan and Iseult found each other again by night and set to conversing, it was a "parlement"; when, through street encounters and the pressure of cicumstances, people gather and start discussing things, it's an "assembly." This is what should be contrasted with the "sovereignty" of general assemblies, with the palaver of parliaments: the rediscovery of the affective charge linked with speech, with *true* speech. The opposite of democracy is not dictatorship, it is truth. It's precisely because they are moments of *truth*, where power is laid bare, that insurrections are never democratic.

3. Without causing any major stir, the "world's greatest democracy" embarked on a global manhunt for one of its agents, Edward Snowden, who had the bad idea of revealing its program of generalized surveillance of communications. In actual fact, most of our precious Western democracies have become unabashed police regimes, whereas most of the police regimes of this period proudly wear the title of "democracy." No one took much offense that a Prime Minister like Papandreou was dismissed without notice for having had the outrageous idea of submitting the policies of his country, that is, of the Troika, to the voters. Moreover, in Europe it has become customary to suspend elections when an uncontrollable outcome is anticipated, or to require citizens to revote when a first vote doesn't produce the result that was counted on by the European Commission. The democrats of the "free world" who strutted twenty years ago ought to be tearing out their hair. Isn't it well known that Google, faced with the scandal of its participation in the espionage program, Prism, was reduced to inviting Henry Kissinger to explain to its workers that they would have to resign themselves, that our "security" came at that price? It's almost comical to imagine the go-to man of all the fascist coups of the 1970s in South America speechifying about democracy in front of the very cool, very "innocent," very "apolitical" employees of the Google headquarters in Silicon Valley.

One is reminded of the statement by Rousseau in *The Social Contract*: "If there were a nation of gods, it would govern itself democratically. A government so perfect is not suited to men." Or the one, more cynical, by Rivarol: "There are two truths that must not be separated in this world: 1. That sovereignty resides in the people. 2. That they must never exercise it."

Edward Bernays, the founder of public relations, began the first chapter of his book *Propaganda*, titled "Organizing Chaos," in this way: "The conscious and intelligent manipulation of the organized habits and opinions of the masses is an important element in a democratic society. Those who manipulate this unseen mechanism of society constitute an invisible government which is the true ruling power of our country." That was in 1928. What one has in mind, basically, when one speaks of democracy, is the equivalence between those who govern and those who are governed, whatever the means by which that equivalence is obtained. Whence the epidemic of hypocrisy and hysteria that afflicts our lands. In a democratic regime, one governs *without really appearing to*. The masters clothe themselves in the attributes of the slave and the slaves believe they are the masters. The former, exercising power on behalf of the happiness of the masses, are condemned to a constant hypocrisy, and the latter, imagining they possess a "purchasing power," "rights," or "opinions" that are trampled on all year round, become hysterics as a result. And because hypocrisy is the bourgeois virtue *par excellence*, something irreparably bourgeois becomes permanently attached to democracy. The popular feeling on this point is not mistaken.

Whether one is an Obama democrat or a fierce proponent of workers' councils, and however one imagines "government of the people by the people," what the question of democracy *overlays* is always the question of government. Its premise, its unthought assumption, is that there must be government. But governing is a quite specific way of exercising power. To govern is not to impose a discipline on a body, it is not to compel respect for the Law in a territory even if that means torturing the violators as under the Ancien Régime. A king reigns. A general commands. A judge judges. Governing is something different. It is managing the behaviors of a population, a multiplicity that one must watch over like a shepherd his flock in order to maximize its potential and guide its freedom. So this means taking into account and shaping its desires, its ways of doing and thinking, its habits, its fears, its dispositions, its milieu. It means deploying a whole ensemble of tactics, of discursive, material, and policing tactics, paying close attention to the people's emotions, with their mysterious oscillations; it is acting to prevent rioting and sedition, based on a constant sensitivity to the affective and political climate. Acting upon the milieu and continually modifying the variables of the latter, acting on some to influence the behavior of the others, to keep control of the flock. In short, it means waging a war that's never called one and doesn't look like one, in almost every sphere of human existence. A war of influence—subtle, psychological, indirect.

What has continued to develop since the 17th century in the West is not state power but, through the construction of national states and now through their deterioration, government *as a specific form of power*. If today the rusty old superstructures of nation states can be allowed to crumble without fear, it's precisely because they must give way to that vaunted "governance"—flexible, plastic, informal, Taoist—which is imposed in every domain, whether it be management of oneself, of relationships, of cities, or of corporations. We others, we revolutionaries, can't keep from feeling that we're losing every battle, one by one, because they are all waged at a level we still haven't gained access to, because we mass our forces around positions already lost, because attacks are conducted where we are not defending ourselves. This is largely the result of our still imagining power in the form of the State, the Law, Discipline, and Sovereignty, when it's as government rather that it continues to advance. We look for power in its solid state when it was a long time ago that power passed into a liquid, if not gaseous, state. Frustrated and baffled, we develop a suspicion of anything still having a definite form—habits, loyalties, rootedness, mastery or logic—when power is manifested rather in the ceaseless dissolution of all forms.

Elections don't have anything particularly democratic about them. For a long time, kings were elected and it's a rare autocrat who will say no to a pleasant little plebiscite here and there. Elections are democratic only in that they make it possible to ensure, not people's participation in government, but a certain *adherence* to it, through the illusion that elections create of people having chosen it to some small extent. "Democracy," wrote Marx, "is the truth of all the forms of the state." He was mistaken. Democracy is the truth *of all the forms of government*. The identity of the governing and the governed is the limit where the flock becomes a collective shepherd and the shepherd dissolves into his flock, where freedom coincides with obedience, the population with the sovereign. The collapsing of governing and governed into each other is government *in its pure state*, with no more form or limit. It's not without reason that *liquid* democracy has begun to be theorized, because every fixed form is an obstacle to the exercise of pure government. In the great movement of general fluidification, there are no stop-blocks, there are only stages on an asymptote. The more fluid it is the more governable it is, and the more governable it is the more democratic it is. The metropolitan single is clearly more democratic than the married couple, which is itself more democratic than the family clan, which is more democratic than the mafia-run neighborhood.

Those who thought that the forms of Law were a definitive acquisition of democracy, and not a transitory form in the process of being outstripped, must be feeling disappointed. Those forms are now a formal hindrance to the elimination of democracy's "enemy combattants" and to the continual reorganization of the economy. From Italy of the 1970s to Obama's dirty wars, antiterrorism is not a regrettable violation of our fine democratic principles, a marginal exception to the latter; it is rather the uninterrupted *constitutive action* by which contemporary democracies are held together. The United States maintains a list of "terrorists" of the entire world containing 680,000 names, and feeds a corps of 25,000 men, the Joint Special Operations Command, secretly charged with going to kill just about anyone at any time anywhere on the surface of the globe. With their fleet of drones that are not so attentive to the exact identity of those they blow to smithereens, extrajudicial executions have supplanted the Guantánamo-type of extrajudicial procedures. Those who raise objections to this don't understand what it means to *govern democratically*. They are stuck in the preceding phase, where the modern state still spoke the language of Law.

In Brazil, under anti-terrorism provisions some young people were arrested whose crime was to have tried to organize a demonstration against the World Cup. In Italy, four comrades were jailed for "terrorism" on the grounds that an attack on the work site of the TAV, the high-speed train line, seriously damaged the country's "image" by burning a compressor. Useless to multiply the examples, the fact is universal: everything that resists the schemes of governments risks being treated as "terrorist." A liberal mind might fear that governments are detracting from their democratic legitimacy. That is not at all the case; in fact, through such a practice they reestablish it. That is, if the operation works. If they've read the prevailing mood correctly and prepared the public sensibility. Because when Ben Ali or Mubarak denounced the crowds filling the streets as terrorist gangs, and that didn't take, the restablishment operation turned back against them. Its failure sucked the ground of legitimacy out from under their feet and they found themselves pedaling above the void, in view of everyone—their downfall was imminent. Such an operation appears for what it is only at the moment it fails.

4. Coming out of Argentina, the slogan "¡Que se vayan todos!" jarred the ruling heads all over the world. There's no counting the number of languages in which we've shouted our desire, during the past few years, to *destitute* the power in place. And the most surprising thing still is that in several cases we managed to do that. But however fragile the regimes succeeding such "revolutions," the second part of the slogan, "¡Y que no quede ni uno!" ("And let not a single one remain!"), has gone unheeded: new puppets have taken the places left vacant. The most exemplary case has to be Egypt. Tahrir had Mubarak's head and the Tamarod movement that of Morsi. Each time, the street demanded a destitution that it didn't have the strength to organize, so that it was the already organized forces, the Muslim Brotherhood then the army, that usurped that destitution and carried it through to their benefit. A movement that demands is always at a disadvantage opposite a force that *acts*. We can marvel in passing at how the role of the sovereign and that of the "terrorist" are basically interchangeable, seeing how quickly one transitions from the palaces of power to the basements of its prisons, and vice versa.

So the complaint that is commonly heard among yesterday's insurgents says: "The revolution was betrayed. We didn't die to make it possible for a provisional government to organize elections, then a constituent assembly to draw up a new constitution that would lay out the modalities of new elections from which a new regime would emerge, which would be almost identical to the previous one. We wanted life to change, and nothing has changed, or very little." On this point, radicals always give the same explanation: it's that the people have to govern themselves instead of electing representatives. If revolutions are consistently betrayed this may be the result of fate, but perhaps it's a sign that some hidden flaws in our idea of revolution condemn it to such an inevitability. One of those flaws is in the fact that we still tend to conceive of revolution as a dialectic between the constituent and the constituted. We still believe in the fable that tells us all constituted power is rooted in a constituent power, that the state emanates from the nation, as the absolute monarch does from God, that beneath the constitution in force there always exists another constitution, an order that's underlying and transcendent at once, silent normally, but capable at certain moments of flashing into presence. We like to think that "the people" only have to assemble, ideally in front of the parliament, and shout "You don't represent us!" for the constituent power to magically depose the constituted powers through its simple epiphany. This fiction of the constituent power actually only serves to mask the strictly political, fortuitous origin, the *raw coup* by which power is instituted. Those who've taken power project the source of their authority back onto the social totality which they henceforth control, and in this way legimately silence it *in its own name*. So it happens that the feat of getting the people fired upon in the name of the people is regularly accomplished. Constituent power is the matador's costume which the squalid origin of power always sports, the veil that hypnotizes everyone and makes them believe that the constituted power is much more than it is.

Those who propose, like Antonio Negri, to "govern the revolution" only see "constituent struggles" everywhere, from the banlieue riots to the uprisings in the Arab world. A Madrid-based Negriist who supports a hypothetical "constituent process" coming out the movement of the squares, even calls for the creation of "the party of democracy," "the party of the 99%," for the purpose of "articulating a new democratic constitution just as 'ordinary,' as non-representative as 15M was." Misdirections of this kind encourage us to reconceive the idea of revolution as *pure destitution* instead.

To institute or constitute a power is to give it a basis, a foundation, a legitimacy. For an economic, judicial, or police apparatus, it is to ground its fragile existence in a dimension that is beyond it, in a transcendence designed to place it out of reach. Through this operation, what is never anything but a localized, specific, partial entity is elevated to an elsewhere from which it can then claim to encompass the whole. As a constituted thing, a power becomes an order with no outside, an uncontested existence with no counterpart, which can only subject or annihilate. The dialectic of the constituent and the constituted comes to confer a higher meaning on what is never anything but a contingent political form. This is how the Republic becomes the universal banner of an indisputable and eternal human nature, or the caliphate the single locus of community. Constituent power names that monstrous piece of magic that turns the state into that entity that's never wrong, having its basis in reason; that has no enemies, since to oppose it is to be a criminal; that can do anything, being without honor.

So to destitute power it's not enough to defeat it in the street, to dismantle its apparatuses, to set its symbols ablaze. To destitute power is to deprive it of its foundation. That is precisely what insurrections do. There the constituted appears as it is, with its thousand maneuvers—clumsy or effective, crude or sophisticated. "The king has no clothes," one says then, because the constituent veil is in tatters and everyone sees through it. To destitute power is to take away its legitimacy, compel it to recognize its arbitrariness, reveal its contingent dimension. It's to show that it holds together only in situation, through what it deploys in the way of stratagems, methods, tricks—to turn it into a temporary configuration of things which, like so many others, have to fight and scheme in order to survive. It's to make the government lower itself to the level of the insurgents, who can no longer be "monsters," "criminals," or "terrorists" but simply enemies. To force the police to be nothing more henceforth than a gang, and the justice system a criminal association. In insurrection, the power in place is just one force among others from the perspective of common struggle, and no longer that meta-force which regiments, commands, or condemns all potentialities. All motherfuckers have addresses. To destitute power is to bring it back down to earth.

Whatever the outcome of the street confrontations, insurrection has always-already torn holes in the tight fabric of beliefs that enable government to be exercised. That is why those in a hurry to bury the insurrection don't waste their time trying to mend the broken foundation of an already invalidated legitimacy. They attempt instead to infuse the movement itself with a new claim to legitimacy, that is, a new claim to be founded on reason, to preside over the strategic plane where the different forces clash. The legitimacy of "the people," "the oppressed," "the 99%" is the Trojan horse by which the constituent is smuggled back into insurrectionary destitution. This is the surest method for undoing an insurrection—one that doesn't even require defeating it in the streets. To make the destitution irreversible, therefore, we must begin by abandoning *our own legitimacy*. We have to give up the idea that one makes the revolution in the name of something, that there's a fundamentally just and innocent entity which the revolutionary forces would have the task of representing. One doesn't bring power back down to earth in order to raise oneself above the heavens.

Destituting this epoch's specific form of power requires, for a start, that one challenge the notion that men need to be governed, either democratically by themselves or hierarchically by others, returning it to its status as a hypothesis, not a "self-evident" truth. The assumption goes back at least to the birth of politics in Greece—its power is such that even the Zapatistas have gathered their "autonomous communes" under the umbrella of "good-government councils." A definite anthropology is at work here, which is found in the anarchist individualist aspiring to the full satisfaction of their personal passions and needs and in seemingly more pessimistic conceptions, seeing man as a voracious beast who can only be kept from devouring his neighbor by a coercive power. Machiavelli, for whom men are "ungrateful, fickle, liars and deceivers, fearful of danger and greedy for gain," is in agreement on this point with the founders of American democracy: "In contriving a system of government, man ought to be supposed a knave," asserted Hamilton. In every case, one starts from the idea that the political order is designed to contain a more or less bestial human nature, where the Self faces the others and the world, where there are only separate bodies that must be bound together through some artifice. As Marshall Sahlins has shown, this idea of a human nature that "culture" must contain is a *Western illusion*. It expresses *our* misery, and not that of all earth dwellers. "For the greater part of humanity, self-interest as we know it is unnatural in the normative sense: it is considered madness, witchcraft or some such grounds for ostracism, execution or at least therapy. Rather than expressing a pre-social human nature, such avarice is generally taken for a loss of humanity."

But in order to destitute government, it's not enough to criticize this anthropology and its presumed "realism." One must find a way to grasp it *from the outside*, to affirm a different plane of perception. For we do move *on a different plane*. From the relative outside of what we're experiencing, of what we're trying to construct, we've arrived at this conviction: the question of government only arises from a void—more often than not, from a void it was obliged to *create*. Power must have sufficiently detached itself from the world, it must have created a sufficient void around the individual, or within him, created a deserted space between beings large enough, so that it becomes a question of organizing all these disparate elements that nothing connects any more, of reassembling the separate elements as separate. Power creates emptiness. Emptiness attracts power.

Leaving the paradigm of government means starting politically from the opposite hypothesis. There is no empty space, everything is inhabited, each one of us is the gathering and crossing point of quantities of affects, lineages, histories, and significations, of material flows that exceed us. The world doesn't environ us, it passes through us. What we inhabit inhabits us. What surrounds us constitutes us. We don't belong to ourselves. We are always-already spread through whatever we attach ourselves to. It's not a question of forming a void from which we could finally manage to catch hold of all that escapes us, but of learning to better inhabit what is there, which implies perceiving it— and there's nothing certain about that for the myopic children of democracy. Perceiving a world peopled not with things but with forces, not with subjects but with powers, not with bodies but with bonds.

It's by virtue of their plenitude that forms of life will complete the destitution.

Here, subtraction is affirmation and affirmation is an element of attack.

Turin, January 28, 2012.

3

POWER IS LOGISTIC.
BLOCK EVERYTHING!

1. *Power Now Resides in Infrastructures.* **2.** *On the Difference Between Organizing and Organizing Oneself.* **3.** *On Blockage.* **4.** *On Investigation.*

1. Occupation of the Kasbah in Tunis and of the Syntagma Square in Athens, siege of Westminster in London during the student movement of 2011, encirclement of the parliament in Madrid on September 25, 2012 or in Barcelona on June 15, 2011, riots all around the Chamber of Deputies in Rome on December 14, 2010, attempt on October 15, 2011 in Lisbon to invade the Assembleia da Republica, burning of the Bosnian presidential residence in February of 2014: the places of institutional power exert a magnetic attraction on revolutionaries. But when the insurgents manage to penetrate parliaments, presidential palaces, and other headquarters of institutions, as in Ukraine, in Libya or in Wisconsin, it's only to discover empty places, that is, empty of power, and furnished without any taste. It's not to prevent the "people" from "taking power" that they are so fiercely kept from invading such places, but to prevent them from realizing that power *no longer resides in the institutions*. There are only deserted temples there, decommissioned fortresses, nothing but stage sets—real traps for revolutionaries. The popular impulse to rush onto the stage to find out what is happening in the wings is bound to be disappointed. If they got inside, even the most fervent conspiracy freaks would find nothing arcane there; the truth is that power is simply no longer that theatrical reality to which modernity accustomed us.

Yet the truth about the actual localization of power is not hidden at all; it's only we who refuse to see it for fear of having our comfortable certainties doused with cold water. For confirmation of this, one only has to look for a moment at the banknotes issued by the European Union. Neither the Marxists nor the neoclassical economists have ever been able to admit that money is not essentially an economic instrument but a political reality. We have never seen any money that was not attached to a political order capable of backing it. That is also why the bills of the different countries bear the personal images of emperors and great statesmen, of founding fathers or personified allegories of the nation. But what is it that appears on euro banknotes? Not human figures, not emblems of a personal sovereignty, but bridges, aqueducts, arches—pieces of impersonal architecture, cold as stone. As to the truth about the present nature of power, every European has a printed exemplar of it in their pocket. It can be stated in this way: *power now resides in the infrastructures of this world.* Contemporary power is of an architectural and impersonal, and not a representative or personal, nature. Traditional power was representative: the pope was the representation of Christ on Earth, the king, of God, the President, of the people, and the General Secretary of the Party, of the proletariat. This whole personal politics is dead, and that is why the small number of orators that survive on the surface of the globe amuse more than they govern. The cast of politicians is actually composed of clowns with varying degrees of talent—whence the phenomenal success of the wretched Beppe Grillo in Italy or the sinister Dieudonné in France. All in all, at least they know how to *entertain* you, which is their profession of course. So, in addition to stating the obvious, reproaching politicians for "not representing us" only maintains a nostalgia. The politicians are not there for that, they're there to distract us, since power is elsewhere. And this correct intuition is what turns nutty in all the contemporary conspiracisms.

Power is indeed somewhere else, somewhere other than in the institutions, but it's not hidden for all that. Or if it is, it's hidden like Poe's "purloined letter." No one sees it because everyone has it in plain sight, all the time—in the form of a high-voltage line, a freeway, a traffic circle, a supermarket, or a computer program. And if it is, it's hidden like a sewage system, an undersea cable, a fiber optic line running the length of a railway, or a data center in the middle of a forest. Power is the very organization of this world, this engineered, configured, *purposed* world. That is the secret, *and it's that there isn't one.*

Power is now immanent in life as it is technologically organized and commodified. It has the neutral appearance of facilities or of Google's blank page. Whoever determines the organization of space, whoever governs the social environments and atmospheres, whoever administers things, whoever manages the accesses—governs men. Contemporary power has made itself the heir, on the one hand, of the old science of policing, which consists in looking after "the well-being and security of the citizens," and, on the other, of the logistic science of militaries, the "art of moving armies," having become an art of maintaining communication networks and ensuring strategic mobility. Absorbed in our language-bound conception of the public thing, of politics, we have continued debating while the real decisions were being implemented *right before our eyes*. Contemporary laws are written in steel structures and not with words. All the citizens' indignation can only end up butting its dazed forehead against the reinforced concrete of this world. The great merit of the struggle against the TAV in Italy is in having firmly grasped all that is involved politically in a simple public works project. Symmetrically, this is something that no politician can acknowledge. Like that Bersani who snapped back one day at the No TAV militants: "After all, we're talking here about a train line, not a bomber." But "a construction site is worth a battalion," in the estimation of Marshal Lyautey, who had no rival in the business of "pacifying" the colonies. If struggles against big infrastructure projects are multiplying all over the world, from Romania to Brazil, it's because this intuition itself is becoming widespread.

Anyone who means to undertake anything whatsoever against the existing world must start from there: the real power structure is the material, technological, physical organization of this world. *Government is no longer in the government.* The "power vacuum" that lasted in Belgium for more than a year is a clear example in point. The country was able to function with no government, elected representatives, parliament, political debate, or electoral issues, without any part of its normal operation being affected. Same thing in Italy, which has been going from "technical government" to "technical government" for years now, and it doesn't bother anyone that this expression goes back to the Manifesto-program of the Futurist Party of 1918, which incubated the first fascists.

Power, henceforth, is the very order of things, and the police charged with defending it. It's not simple to think about a power that consists in infrastructures, in the means to make them function, to control them and to build them. How do we contest an order that isn't articulated in language, that is constructed step by step and wordlessly? An order that is embodied in the very objects of everyday life. An order whose political constitution is its material constitution. An order that is revealed less in the President's words than in the silence of optimal performance. In the age when power manifested itself through edicts, laws, and regulations, it was vulnerable to critical attack. But there's no criticizing a wall, one destroys it or tags it. A government that *arranges* life through its instruments and its layouts, whose statements take the form of a street lined with traffic cones and surveilled by overhead cameras, may only invite a destruction that is wordless itself. Aggression against the setting of everyday life has become sacrilegious, consequently; it's something like violating its constitution. Indiscriminate smashing in urban riots expresses both an awareness of this state of things, and a relative powerlessness in the face of it. The mute and unquestionable order which the existence of a bus shelter embodies will not lie shattered on the ground, unfortunately, once the shelter is demolished. The theory of broken panes will still stand after all the shop windows have been smashed. All the hypocritical proclamations about the sacred character of the "environment," the holy crusade for its defense, can only be understood in light of this mutation: *power has become environmental itself, has merged into the surroundings*. It is power that we're asked to defend in all the official appeals to "preserve the environment," and not the little fish.

2. Everyday life has not always been *organized*. For that to be accomplished, it was necessary first to dismantle life, starting with the city. Life and the city have been broken down into *functions*, corresponding to "social needs." The office district, the factory district, the residential district, the spaces for relaxation, the entertainment district, the place where one eats, the place where one works, the place where one cruises, and the car or bus for tying all that together are the result of a prolonged reconfiguration of life that devastated every form of life. It was carried out methodically, for more than a century, by a whole caste of *organizers*, a

whole grey armada of managers. Life and humanity were dissected into a set of needs; then a synthesis of these elements was organized. It doesn't really matter whether this synthesis was given the name of "socialist planning" or "market planning." It doesn't really matter that it resulted in the failure of new towns or the success of trendy districts. The outcome is the same: a desert and existential anemia. Nothing is left of a form of life once it has been partitioned into organs. Conversely, this explains the palpable joy that overflowed the occupied squares of the Puerta del Sol, Tahrir, Gezi or the attraction exerted, despite the infernal muds of the Nantes countryside, by the land occupation at Notre-Dame-des-Landes. It is the joy that attaches to every commune. Suddenly, life ceases being sliced up into connected segments. Sleeping, fighting, eating, taking care of oneself, partying, conspiring, discussing all belong to the same vital movement. Not everything is *organized*, everything *organizes itself*. The difference is meaningful. One requires management, the other attention—dispositions that are incompatible in every respect.

Referring to the Aymara uprisings in Bolivia at the beginning of the 2000s, a Uruguayan activist, Raúl Zibechi, writes: "In these movements, organization is not separate from daily life. In insurrectionary action it is daily life itself that is deployed." He observes that in the neighborhoods of El Alto, in 2003, "a communal ethos replaced the old trade-union ethos." Very cool, that, because it clarifies what a struggle against infrastructural power consists in. Say infrastructure and you're saying that life has been detached from its conditions. That *conditions have been placed* on life. That life now depends on factors out of its control, that it has lost its footing. Infrastructures organize a life without a world, suspended, expendable, at the mercy of whoever is managing them. Metropolitan nihilism is only a brash way of not admitting this to oneself. Contrariwise, Raúl's statement also indicates what is being sought in the experiments that are underway in a large number of neighborhoods and villages throughout the world, and the inevitable pitfalls. Not a return to earth but a reinhabiting *of* earth. What gives insurrections their punch, and their ability to damage the adversary's infrastructure in a sustained way, is precisely their level of self-organization of communal life. That one of the first reflexes of Occupy Wall Street was to go block the Brooklyn Bridge or that the Oakland Commune along with several thousand people undertook to paralyze the city's port during the general strike of December 12, 2011, are evidence of the intuitive link between self-organization and blockage. The fragility of the self-organization that barely took shape in the occupations did not allow these attempts to be pushed further, apparently. By contrast, Tahrir and Taksim squares are central hubs of automobile circulation in Cairo and Istanbul. To block those flows was to open up the situation. The occupation was immediately a blockade. Hence its ability to throw the reign of normality out of joint in a whole metropolis. At a completely different level, one can't help but draw a connection between the fact that the Zapatistas are currently proposing to link together twenty-nine defensive struggles against mining, highway, power-plant, and dam projects involving different indigenous peoples all over Mexico, and the fact that they themselves have spent the past fifteen years establishing their autonomy vis-à-vis the federal and economic powers.

3. A 2006 sign posted by the French movement against the "first employment contract," the CPE, said: "It's through flows that this world is maintained. Block everything!" This rallying cry, propagated by a minority of a movement that was itself minoritarian, albeit "victorious," has enjoyed a successful run since then. In 2009, the movement against "pwofitasyon," which paralyzed all of Guadaloupe, used it in a big way. And we have seen the practice of blockading, during the French movement against retirement restructuring, become

the staple tactic of struggle, applied uniformly to a fuel depot, a mall, a train station, or a production site. Now, there is something, surely, that reveals a certain state of the world.

The fact that this movement against the overhaul of retirement centered around the blockading of refineries is not politically negligible. At the end of the seventies, refineries became the vanguard of what were called "process industries," "flux" industries. It can be said that refinery operation has served as the model for the restructuring of most factories since that time. Moreover, one should not talk about factories any longer, but about *sites*, production sites. The difference between the factory and the site is that a factory is a concentration of workers, technical know-how, primary materials, stocks, whereas the site is only a node on a map of productive flows. Their only shared trait being that what comes out of both, compared with what went in, has undergone a certain transformation. The refinery is that place where the relation between labor and production was first overturned. There the worker, or rather the operator, doesn't even have the job of maintaining and repairing the machines, which is generally assigned to temporary workers, but simply of bringing a certain attention, a certain vigilance to bear on a totally automated production process. There may be an indicator light that switches on when it shouldn't, an abnormal gurgling in a pipe, smoke escaping where there shouldn't be any, or that doesn't look the way it should. The refinery worker is a kind of monitor of machines, an idle figure, full of nervous concentration. And this is the trend now in most sectors of industry in the West. The classic worker could be gloriously imagined as the Producer; here *the relationship between labor and production is simply inverted.* There is work only when production stops, when a malfunction gets in the way. The Marxists can stick to their day jobs: the process of commodity valorization, from extraction to the pump, coincides with the process of circulation, which itself coincides with the process of production. It depends in real time on the final fluctuations of the market. Saying that the value of the commodity crystallizes the labor time of the worker was a political operation that was as fruitful as it was fallacious. In refineries just as in any completely automated factory, it has become a mark of hurtful irony. Give China ten more years, ten years of workers' demands, and it will be the same situation there. Obviously, it's not insignificant that refinery workers have long been among the best paid industrial workers, and that it was in this sector, at least in France, that what is euphemistically called the "fluidification of social relations," union relations in particular, was first tried out.

During the movement against retirement reform, most of France's fuel depots were blockaded not by their five workers, but by teachers, students, drivers, railroad men, postal employees, unemployed people, and high school students. This wasn't because those industry workers don't have the right. It's simply that in a world where the organization of production is decentralized, fluid, and largely automated, where each machine is now but a link in an integrated system of machines that subsume it, and where this system-world of machines, of machines producing machines, tends to be unified cybernetically, each particular flow is a moment of the overall reproduction of capital's society. There is no longer a "sphere of reproduction" of labor power and social relations distinct from the sphere of production, which itself is no longer a sphere, but rather the web of the world with all its relations. To physically attack these flows, at any point, is therefore to politically attack the system as a whole. If the subject of the strike was the working class, the subject of the blockade is whoever. It's anyone at all, anyone who takes a stand against the existing organization of the world.

It's generally when they reach their maximun degree of sophistication that civilizations fall apart. Every production chain is now reaching such a level of specialization through so many intermediaries that if one of them disappeared that would be enough to paralyze, or even destroy, the whole chain. Three years ago, Honda factories in Japan went through the longest period of layoffs since the sixties simply because the supplier of a particular computer chip had disappeared in the earthquake of March, 2011 and no one else could produce it.

In this blockading craze that now accompanies every movement of any size, we cannot help but read a reversal of our relation to time. We look toward the future in the same way Walter Benjamin's Angel of History looked toward the past. "Where *we* see the appearance of a chain of events, *he* sees one single catastrophe, which unceasingly piles rubble on top of rubble and hurls it before his feet." The time that's passing is longer seen as anything but a slow progression towards an end that will likely be horrendous. Every coming decade looks like another step closer to the climate chaos that everyone has understood to be the truth lurking in the insipid phrase "climate warming." The heavy metals will continue, day by day, to accumulate in the food chain, along with radioactive nuclides and all the other invisible but fatal pollutants. So every attempt to block the global system, every movement, every revolt, every uprising should be seen as a vertical attempt to *stop time*, delay the catastrophe and begin to branch off in a less fatal direction.

4. It's not the weakness of our struggles that explains the disappearance of any revolutionary perspective; it's the absence of any credible revolutionary perspective that explains the weakness of our struggles. Obsessed as we are with a political idea of the revolution, we have neglected its technical dimension. *A revolutionary perspective no longer focuses on an institutional reorganization of society, but on the technical configuration of worlds.* As such, it is a line traced in the present, not an image floating in the future. If we want to regain a perspective, we have to couple the vague awareness that this world can't last with the desire to build a better one. For if this world keeps going, it's largely owing to everyone's material dependence on the smooth general operation of the social machine for their survival. We need to have a technical knowledge of the organization of this world at our disposal; a knowledge that enables us both to neutralize the dominant structures and to secure the necessary time for organizing a material and political disengagement from the general course of the catastrophe, a disengagement not haunted by the specter of extreme poverty, by the urgency of survival. To say that plainly: so long as we can't do without nuclear power plants and dismantling them remains a business for people who want them to last forever, aspiring to abolish the state will continue to draw smiles; so long as the prospect of a popular uprising will signify a guaranteed fall into scarcity, of health care, food, or energy, there will be no strong mass movement. In other words: we need to resume a meticulous effort of investigation. We need to go look in every sector, in all the territories we inhabit, for those who possess strategic technical knowledge. Only on this basis will movements truly dare to "block everything." Only on this basis will the passion for experimenting towards another life be liberated, a largely technical passion that is the obverse, as it were, of everyone's state of technological dependence. This process of knowledge accumulation, of establishing collusions in every domain, is a prerequisite for a serious and massive return of the revolutionary question.

"The workers' movement wasn't defeated by capitalism, but by democracy," said Mario Tronti. It was also defeated by failing to appropriate the substance of working-class power. What defines the worker is not his exploitation by a boss, which he shares with all other employees. What distinguishes him in a positive sense is his embodied technical mastery of a particular world of production. There is a competence in this that is scientific and popular at the same time, a passionate knowledge that constituted the particular wealth of the working world before capital, realizing the danger contained there and having first extracted all that knowledge, decided to turn workers into operators, monitors, and custodians of machines. But even there, the workers' power remains: someone who knows how to make a system operate also knows how to sabotage it in an effective way. But no one can individually master the set of techniques that enable the current system to reproduce itself. Only a collective force can do that. This is exactly what it means to construct a revolutionary force today: linking together all the worlds and all the revolutionarily necessary techniques, shaping these into a historical force and not a system of government.

The failure of the French struggle against retirement restructuring in the autumn of 2010 taught a bitter lesson on this subject. If the CGT had control of the whole struggle, it was due to our inadequacy in the technical sphere. All the union needed to do was turn the blockade of the refineries, where it was hegemonic, into the spearhead of the movement. That way it was free at any moment to signal the end of the game by reopening the refinery valves, thereby releasing all the pressure on the country. What the movement lacked at that point was precisely a minimal knowledge of the material functioning of that world, a knowledge scattered among some workers, concentrated in the egghead brains of a few engineers, and shared no doubt, on the opposing side, in some obscure military agency. If we had been able to cut off the police's supply of teargas, or interrupt the televised propaganda for a day, or deprive the authorities of electricity, we can be sure that things would not have ended so pitifully. Moreover, it has to be concluded that the main *political* defeat of the movement was to have surrendered the strategic prerogative of deciding *who* would have gasoline and *who* would not to the State, with its requisitions at the prefectural level.

"Nowadays if you want to get rid of someone, you go after his infrastructure," writes an American academic, incisively. Since the Second World War, the American Air Force has been developing the idea of "infrastructure warfare," seeing the most ordinary civil infrastructure as targets for bringing its opponents to their knees. This explains, in fact, why strategic infrastructure facilities are enveloped in a growing secrecy. For a revolutionary force there is no sense in its knowing how to block the opponent's infrastructure if it can't make such facilities operate for its benefit if there's a need. Being able to destroy the technological system presupposes that one has tried out/ implemented the techniques that make the system superfluous. Reinhabiting the earth means, to start with, no longer living in ignorance of the conditions of our existence.

4

FUCK OFF, GOOGLE

1. There Are No "Facebook Revolutions," but There Is a New "Science of Government," Cybernetics. 2. A Curse on All Things Smart! 3. The Poverty of Cybernetics. 4. Techniques against Technology.

1. The genealogy is not well known, and it deserves to be. Twitter descends from a program named TXTMob, invented by American activists as a way to coordinate via cellphones during protests against the Republican National Convention in 2004. The application was used by some 5000 people to share real-time information about the different actions and movements of the police. Twitter, launched two years later, was used for similar purposes, in Moldova for example, and the Iranian demonstrations of 2009 popularized the idea that it was the tool for coordinating insurgents, particularly against dictatorships. In 2011,

Oakland, December 20, 2013.

when rioting reached an England thought to be definitively impassive, some journalists were sure that tweeting had helped spread the disturbances from their epicenter, Tottenham. Logical, but it turned out that for their communication needs the rioters had gone with BlackBerry, whose secure telephones had been designed for the upper management of banks and multinationals, and the British secret service didn't even have the decryption keys for them. Moreover, a group of hackers hacked into BlackBerry's site to dissuade the company from cooperating with the police in the aftermath. If Twitter enabled a self-organization on this occasion it was more that of the citizen sweepers who volunteered to sweep up and repair the damage caused by the confrontations and looting. That effort was relayed and coordinated by CrisisCommons, a "global network of volunteers [...] working together to build and use technology tools to help respond to disasters and improve resiliency and response before a crisis." At the time, a French left-wing rag compared this undertaking to the organization of the Puerta del Sol during the Indignants Movement, as it's called. The comparison between a scheme aimed at a quick return to order and the fact of several thousand people organizing to live on an occupied plaza, in the face of repeated assaults by the police, may look absurd. Unless we see in them just two *spontaneous, connected, civic gestures.* From 15-M on, the Spanish "indignados," a good number of them at least, called attention to their faith in a citizens' utopia. For them the digital social networks had not only accelerated the spread of the 2011 movement, but also and more importantly had set the terms of a new type of political organization, for the struggle and for society: a connected, participatory, transparent democracy. It's bound to be upsetting for "revolutionaries" to share such an idea with Jared Cohen, the American government's anti-terrorism adviser who contacted Twitter during the "Iranian revolution" of 2009 and urged them to maintain it's functioning despite censorship. Jared Cohen has recently cowritten with Google's former CEO, Eric Schmidt, a creepy political book, *The New Digital Age.* On its first page one reads this sentence meant to maintain the confusion about the political virtues of the new communication technologies: "The Internet is the largest experiment involving anarchy in history."

"In Tripoli, Tottenham or Wall Street people have been protesting failed policies and the meager possibilities afforded by the electoral system… They have lost faith in government and other centralized institutions of power… There is no viable justification for a democratic system in which public participation is limited to voting. We live in a world in which ordinary people write

Wikipedia; get online to help organize a protest in cyberspace and in the physical world, such as the revolutions in Egypt or Tunisia or the demonstrations of the 'indignados' throughout Spain; or pore over the cables revealed by WikiLeaks. The same technologies enabling us to work together at a distance are creating the expectation to do better at governing ourselves." This is not an "*indignada*" speaking, or if so, she's one who camped for a long time in an office of the White House: Beth Noveck directed the "Open Government Initiative" of the Obama administration. That program starts from the premise that the governmental function should consist in linking up citizens and making available information that's now held inside the bureaucratic machine. Thus, according to New York's city hall, "the hierarchical structure based on the notion that the government knows what's good for you is outdated. The new model for this century depends on co-creation and collaboration."

Unsurprisingly, the concept of Open Government Data was formulated not by politicians but by computer programmers—fervent defenders of open source software development, moreover—who invoked the US founding fathers' conviction that "every citizen should take part in government." Here the government is reduced to the role of team leader or facilitator, ultimately to that of a "platform for coordinating citizen action." The parallel with social networks is fully embraced. "How can the city think of itself in the same way Facebook has an API ecosystem or Twitter does?" is the question on their minds at the New York mayor's office. "This can enable us to produce a more user-centric experience of government. It's not just the consumption but the co-production of government services and democracy." Even if these declarations are seen as fanciful cogitations, as products of the somewhat overheated brains of Silicon Valley, they still confirm that the practice of government is less and less identified with state sovereignty. In the era of networks, governing means ensuring the interconnection of people, objects, and machines as well as the free—i.e., transparent and controllable—circulation of information that is generated in this manner. This is an activity already conducted largely outside the state apparatuses, even if the latter try by every means to maintain control of it. It's becoming clear that Facebook is not so much the model of a new form of government as its reality already in operation. The fact that revolutionaries employed it and still employ it to link up in the street en masse only proves that it's possible, in some places, to use Facebook against itself, against its essential function, which is policing.

When computer scientists gain entry, as they're doing, into the presidential palaces and mayors' offices of the world's largest cities, it's not so much to set up shop as it is to explain the new rules of the game: government administrations are now competing with alternative providers of the same services who, unfortunately for them, are several steps ahead. Suggesting their cloud as a way to shelter government services from revolutions—services like the land registry, soon to be available as a smartphone application—the authors of *The New Digital Age* inform us and them: "In the future, people won't just back up their data; they'll back up their government." And in case it's not quite clear who the boss is now, it concludes: "Governments may collapse and wars can destroy physical infrastructure but virtual institutions will survive." With Google, what is concealed beneath the exterior of an innocent interface and a very effective search engine, is an explicitly political project. An enterprise that maps the planet Earth, sending its teams into every street of every one of its towns, cannot have purely commercial aims. One never maps a territory that one doesn't contemplate appropriating. "Don't be evil." = "Leave everything to us."

It's a little troubling to note that under the tents that covered Zuccotti Park and in the offices of planning—a little higher in the New York sky—the response to disaster is conceived in the same terms: connection, networking, self-organization.

This is a sign that at the same time that the new communication technologies were put into place that would not only weave their web over the Earth but form the very texture of the world in which we live, a certain way of thinking and of governing was in the process of winning. Now, the basic principles of this new science of government were framed by the same ones, engineers and scientists, who invented the technical means of its application. The history is as follows. In the 1940s, while he was finishing his work for the American army, the mathematician Norbert Wiener undertook to establish both a new science and a new definition of man, of his relationship with the world and with himself. Claude Shannon, an engineer at Bell and MIT, whose work on sampling theory contributed to the development of telecommunications, took part in this project. As did the amazing Gregory Bateson, a Harvard anthropologist, employed by the American secret service in Southeast Asia during the Second World War, a sophisticated fan of LSD and founder of the Palo Alto School. And there was the truculent John von Neumann, writer of the *First Draft of a Report on the EDVAC*, regarded as the founding text of computer science—the inventor of game theory, a decisive contribution to neoliberal economics—a proponent of a preventive nuclear strike against the USSR, and who, after having determined the optimal points for releasing the Bomb on Japan, never tired of rendering various services to the American army and the budding CIA. Hence the very persons who made substantial contributions to the new means of communication and to data processing after the Second World War also laid the basis of that "science" that Wiener called "cybernetics." A term that Ampère, a century before, had had the good idea of defining as the "science of government." So we're talking about an art of governing whose formative moments are almost forgotten but whose concepts branched their way underground, feeding into information technology as much as biology, artificial intelligence, management, or the cognitive sciences, at the same time as the cables were strung one after the other over the whole surface of the globe.

We're not undergoing, since 2008, an abrupt and unexpected "economic crisis," we're only witnessing the slow collapse of political economy *as an art of governing*. Economics has never been a reality or a science; from its inception in the 17th century, it's never been anything but an art of governing populations. Scarcity had to be avoided if riots were to be avoided—hence the importance of "grains"—and wealth was to be produced to increase the power of the sovereign. "The surest way for all government is to rely on the interests of men," said Hamilton. Once the "natural" laws of economy were elucidated, governing meant letting its harmonious mechanism operate freely and moving men by manipulating their interests. Harmony, the predictability of behaviors, a radiant future, an assumed rationality of the actors: all this implied a certain trust, the ability to "give credit." Now, it's precisely these tenets of the old governmental practice which management through permanent crisis is pulverizing. We're not experiencing a "crisis of trust" but the *end* of trust, which has become superfluous to government. Where control and transparency reign, where the subjects' behavior is anticipated in real time through the algorithmic processing of a mass of available data about them, there's no more need to trust them or for them to trust. It's sufficient that they be sufficiently monitored. As Lenin said, "Trust is good, control is better."

The West's crisis of trust in itself, in its knowledge, in its language, in its reason, in its liberalism, in its subject and in the world, actually dates back to the end of the 19th century; it breaks forth in every domain with and around the First World War. Cybernetics developed on that open wound of modernity. It asserted itself as a remedy for the existential and thus governmental crisis of the West. As Norbert Wiener saw it, "We are shipwrecked passengers on a doomed planet. Yet even in a shipwreck, human decencies and human values do not necessarily vanish, and we must make the most of them. We shall go down, but let it be in a manner to which we may look forward as worthy of our dignity." Cybernetic government is inherently apocalyptic. Its purpose is to locally impede the spontaneously entropic, chaotic movement of the world and to ensure "enclaves of order," of stability, and—who knows?—the perpetual self-regulation of systems, through the unrestrained, transparent, and controllable circulation of information. "Communication is the cement of society and those whose work consists in keeping the channels of communication open are the ones on whom the continuance or downfall of our civilization largely depends," declared Wiener, believing he knew. As in every period of transition, the changeover from the old economic governmentality to cybernetics included a phase of instability, a historical opening where governmentality *as such* risked being put in check.

2. In the 1980s, Terry Winograd, the mentor of Larry Page, one of the founders of Google, and Fernando Flores, the former finance minister of Salvador Allende, wrote concerning design in information technology that "the most important designing is ontological. It constitutes an intervention in the background of our heritage, growing

out of our already existent ways of being in the world, and deeply affecting the kinds of beings that we are [...] It is necessarily reflective and political." The same can be said of cybernetics. Officially, we continue to be governed by the old dualistic Western paradigm where there is the subject and the world, the individual and society, men and machines, the mind and the body, the living and the nonliving. These are distinctions that are still generally taken to be valid. In reality, cybernetized capitalism does practice an ontology, and hence an anthropology, whose key elements are reserved for its initiates. The rational Western subject, mindful of his interests, aspiring to master the world and governable thereby, gives way to the cybernetic conception of a being without an interiority, of a selfless self, an emergent, climatic being, constituted by its exteriority, by its relations. A being which, armed with its Apple Watch, comes to understand itself entirely on the basis of external data, the statistics that each of its behaviors generates. A Quantified Self that is will monitor, measure, and desperately optimize every one of its gestures and each of its affects. For the most advanced cybernetics, there's already no longer man and his environment, but a system-being which is itself part of an ensemble of complex information systems, hubs of autonomic processes— a being that can be better explained by starting from the middle way of Indian Buddhism than from Descartes. "For man, being alive means the same thing as participating in a broad global system of communication," asserted Wiener in 1948.

Just as political economy produced a *homo economicus* manageable in the framework of industrial States, cybernetics is producing its own humanity. A transparent humanity, emptied out by the very flows that traverse it, electrified by information, attached to the world by an ever-growing quantity of apparatuses. A humanity that's inseparable from its technological environment because it is constituted, and thus driven, by that. Such is the object of government now: no longer man or his interests, but his "social environment." An environment whose model is the smart city. Smart because by means of its sensors it produces information whose processing in real time makes self-management possible. And smart because it produces and is produced by smart inhabitants. Political economy reigned over beings by leaving them free to pursue their interest; cybernetics controls them by leaving them free to communicate. "We need to reinvent the social systems in a controlled framework," some MIT professor declared recently.

The most petrifying and most realistic vision of the metropolis to come is not found in the brochures that IBM distributes to municipalities to sell them software for managing the flows of water, electricity, or road traffic. It's rather the one developed in principle "against" that Orwellian vision of the city: "smarter cities" coproduced by their residents themselves (in any case by the best connected among them). Another MIT professor traveling in Catalonia is pleased to see its capital becoming little by little a "fab city": "Sitting here right in the heart of Barcelona I see a new city being invented where everyone will have access to the tools to make it completely autonomous." The citizens are thus no longer subalterns but *smart people*, "receivers and generators of ideas, services, and solutions," as one of them says. In this vision, the metropolis doesn't become smart through the decision-making and action of a central government, but appears, as a "spontaneous order," when its inhabitants "find new ways of producing, connecting, and giving meaning to their own data." The *resilient* metropolis thus emerges, one that can resist every disaster.

Behind the futuristic promise of a world of fully linked people and objects, when cars, fridges, watches, vacuums, and dildos are directly connected to each other and to the Internet, there is what is already here: the fact that the most polyvalent of sensors is already in operation: myself. "I" share my geolocation, my mood, my opinions, my account of what I saw today that was awesome or awesomely banal. I ran, so I immediately shared my route, my time, my performance numbers and their self-evaluation. I always post photos of my vacations, my evenings, my riots, my colleagues, of what I'm going to eat and who I'm going to fuck. I appear not to do much and yet I produce a steady stream of data. Whether I work or not, my everyday life, as a stock of information, can always be mined. I am constantly improving the algorithm.

"Thanks to the widespread networks of sensors, we will have a God's eye view of ourselves. For the first time, we can precisely map the behavior of masses of people at the level of their daily lives," enthuses one of the professors. The great refrigerated storehouses of data are the pantry of current government. In its rummaging through the databases produced and continuously updated by the everyday life of connected humans, it looks for the correlations it can use to establish not universal laws nor even "whys," but rather "whens" and "whats," one-time, situated predictions, not to say oracles. The stated ambition of cybernetics is to manage the unforeseeable, and to govern the ungovernable instead of trying to destroy it. The question of cybernetic government is not only, as in the era of political economy, to anticipate in order to plan the action to take, but also to act directly upon the virtual, to structure the possibilities. A few years ago, the LAPD bought itself a new software program called PredPol. Based on a heap of crime statistics, it calculates the probabilities that a particular crime will be committed, neighborhood by neighborhood, street by street. Given these probabilities updated in real time, the program itself organizes the police patrols in the city. A founder cybernetician wrote in *Le Monde* in 1948: "We can dream of a time when the *machine à gouverner* will—for good or evil, who knows?—compensate for the shortcomings, obvious today, of the leaders and customary apparatuses of politics." Every epoch dreams the next one, even if the dream of the one may become the daily nightmare of the other.

The object of the great harvest of personal information is not an individualized tracking of the whole population. If the surveillants insinuate themselves into the intimate lives of each and every person, it's not so much to construct individual files as to assemble massive databases that make numerical sense. It is more efficient to correlate the shared characteristics of individuals in a multitude of "profiles," with the probable developments they suggest. One is not interested in the individual, present and entire, but only in what makes it possible to determine their potential lines of flight. The advantage of applying the surveillance to profiles, "events," and virtualities is that statistical entities don't take offense, and individuals can still claim they're not being monitored, at least not personally. While cybernetic governmentality already operates in terms of a completely new logic, its subjects continue to think of themselves according to the old paradigm. We believe that our "personal" data belong to us, like our car or our shoes, and that we're only exercising our "individual freedom" by deciding to let Google, Facebook, Apple, Amazon or the police have access to them, without realizing that this has immediate effects on those who refuse to, and who will be treated from then on as suspects, as potential deviants. "To be sure," predicts *The New Digital Age*, "there will be people who resist adopting and using technology, people who want nothing to do with virtual pro-files, online data systems or smart phones. Yet a government might suspect that people who opt out completely have something to hide and thus are more likely to break laws, and as a counterterrorism measure, that government will build [a] kind of 'hidden people' registry [...] If you don't have any registered social-networking profiles or mobile subscriptions, and on-line references to you are unusually hard to find, you might be considered a candidate for such a registry. You might also be subjected to a strict set of new regulations that includes rigorous airport screening or even travel restrictions."

3. So the security services are coming to consider a Facebook profile more *credible* than the individual supposedly hiding behind it. This is some indication of the porousness between what was still called the virtual and the real. The accelerating datafication of the world does make it less and less pertinent to think of the online world and the real world, cyberspace and reality, as being separate. "Look at Android, Gmail, Google Maps, Google Search. That's what we do. We make products that people can't live without," is how they put it in Mountain View. Yet, in the past few years, the ubiquity of connected devices in the everyday lives of human beings has triggered some survival reflexes. Certain barkeepers decided to ban Google Glasses from their establishments—which became truly hip as a result, it should be said. Initiatives are blossoming that encourage people to disconnect occasionally (one day per week, for a weekend, a month) in order to take note of their dependence on technological objects and re-experience an "authentic" contact with reality. The attempt proves to be futile of course. The pleasant weekend at the seashore with one's family and without the smartphones is lived primarily *as an experience of disconnection*; that is, as something immediately anticipating the moment of reconnection, when it will be shared on the Internet.

Eventually, however, with Western man's abstract relation to the world becoming objectified in a whole complex of apparatuses, a whole universe of virtual reproductions, the path towards presence paradoxically reopens. By detaching ourselves from everything, we'll end up detaching ourselves even from our detachment. The technological beat-down will ultimately restore our capacity to be moved by the bare, pixelless existence of a honey-suckle vine. Every sort of screen coming between us and reality will have been required before we could reclaim the singular shimmer of the sensible world, and our amazement at what is there. It will have taken hundreds of "friends" who have nothing to do with us, "liking" us on Facebook the better to ridicule us afterwards, for us to rediscover the ancient taste for friendship.

Having failed to create computers capable of equaling human beings, they've set out to impoverish human experience to the point where life is no more attractive than its digital modeling. Can one picture the human desert that had to be created to make existence on the social media seem desirable? Just as the traveler had to be replaced by the tourist for it to be imagined that the latter might pay to go all over the world via hologram while remaining in their living room. But the slightest real experience will shatter the wretchedness of this kind of illu-sionism. *The poverty of cybernetics is what will bring it down in the end.* For a hyper-individualized generation whose primary sociality had been that of the social media, the Quebec student strike of 2012 was first of all a stunning revelation of the insurrectionary power of simply being together and starting to move. Evidently, this was a meet-up like no other before, such that the insurgent friendships were able to rush the police lines. The control traps were useless against that; in fact, they had become another way for people to test themselves, together. "The end of the Self will be the genesis of presence," envisioned Giorgio Cesarano in his *Survival Manual.*

The virtue of the hackers has been to base themselves on the materiality of the supposedly virtual world. In the words of a member of Telecomix, a group of hackers famous for helping the Syrians get around the state control of Internet communications, if the hacker is ahead of his time it's because he "didn't think of this tool [the Internet] as a separate virtual world but as an extension of physical reality." This is all the more obvious now that the hacker movement is extending itself outside the screens by opening hackerspaces where people can analyze, tinker with, and piece together digital software and tech objects. The expansion and networking of Do It Yourself has produced a gamut of purposes: it's a matter of fooling with things, with the street, the city, the society, life itself. Some pathological progressives have been quick to see the beginnings of a new economy in it, even a new civilization, based this time on "sharing." Never mind that the present capitalist economy already values "creation," beyond the old industrial constraints. Managers are urged to facilitate free initiative, to encourage innovative projects, creativity, genius, even deviance—"the company of the future must protect the deviant, for it's the deviant who will innovate and who is capable of creating rationality in the unknown," they say. Today, value is not sought in the new features of a product, nor even in its desirability or its meaning, but in the experience it offers to the consumer. So why not offer that consumer the ultimate experience of going over to the other side of the creation process? From this perspective, the hackerspaces or "fablabs" become spaces where the "projects" of "consumer-innovators" can be undertaken and "new marketplaces" can emerge. In San Francisco, the TechShop firm is developing a new type of fitness club where, for a yearly membership fee, "one goes every week to make things, to create and develop one's projects."

The fact that the American army finances similar places under the Cyber Fast Track program of DARPA (Defense Advanced Research Project Agency) doesn't discredit the hackerspaces as such. Any more than they're condemned to participate in yet another restructuring of the capitalist production process when they're captured in the "Maker" movement with its spaces where people working together can build and repair industrial objects or divert them from their original uses. Village construction sets, like that of Open Source Ecology with its fifty modular machines—tractor, milling machine, cement mixer, etc.—and DIY dwelling modules could also have a different destiny than serving to found a "small civilization with all the modern comforts," or creating "entire new economies" or a "financial system" or a "new governance," as its current guru fantasizes. Urban farming which is being established on building roofs or vacant industrial lots, like the 1300 community gardens of Detroit, could have other ambitions than participating in economic recovery or bolstering the "resilience of disaster zones." Attacks like those conducted by Anonymous/LulzSec against the police, banking firms, security multinationals, or telecommunications could very well go beyond cyberspace. As a Ukrainian hacker says, "When you have to attend to your life, you stop printing stuff in 3D rather quickly. You find a different plan."

4. The famous "question concerning technology," still a blind spot for revolutionary movements, comes in here. A wit whose name can be forgotten described the French tragedy thus: "a generally

technophobic country dominated by a generally technophilic elite." While the observation may not apply to the country, it does apply in any case to the radical milieus. The majority of Marxists and post-Marxists supplement their atavistic inclination to hegemony with a definite attachment to technology-that-emancipates-man, whereas a large percentage of anarchists and post-anarchists are down with being a minority, even an oppressed minority, and adopt positions generally hostile to "technology." Each tendency even has its caricature: corresponding to the Negriist devotees of the cyborg, the electronic revolution by connected multitudes, there are the anti-industrials who've turned the critique of progress and the "disaster of technological civilization" into a profitable literary genre on the whole, and a niche ideology where one can stay warm at least, having envisaged no revolutionary possibility whatsoever. Technophilia and technophobia form a diabolical pair joined together by a central untruth: that such a thing as the technical exists. It would be possible, apparently, to divide between what is technical and what is not, in human existence. Well, no, in fact. One only has to look at the state of incompletion in which the human offspring is born, and the time it takes for it to move about in the world and to talk, to realize that its relation to the world is not given in the least, but rather the result of a whole elaboration. Since it's not due to a natural compatibility, man's relation to the world is essentially artificial, *technical*, to speak Greek. Each human world is a certain configuration of techniques, of culinary, architectural, musical, spiritual, informational, agricultural, erotic, martial, etc., techniques. And it's for this reason that there's no generic human essence: because there are only particular techniques, and because every technique configures a world, materializing in this way a certain relationship with the latter, a certain *form of life*. So one doesn't "construct" a form of life; one only incorporates techniques, through example, exercise, or apprenticeship. This is also why our familiar world rarely appears to us as "technical": because the set of artifices that structure it are already part of us. It's rather those we're not familiar with that seem to have a strange artificiality. Hence the technical character of our world only stands out in two circumstances: invention and "breakdown." It's only when we're present at a discovery or when a familiar element is lacking, or breaks, or stops functioning, that the illusion of living in a natural world gives way in the face of contrary evidence.

Techniques can't be reduced to a collection of equivalent instruments any one of which Man, that generic being, could take up and use without his essence being affected. Every tool configures and embodies a particular relation with the world, and influences the one who uses it. The worlds formed in this way are not equivalent, any more than the humans who inhabit them are. And by the same token these worlds are not hierarchizable either. There is nothing that would establish some as more "advanced" than others. They are merely distinct, each one having its own potential and its own history. In order to hierarchize worlds a criterion has to be introduced, an implicit criterion making it possible to classify the different techniques. In the case of progress, this criterion is simply the quantifiable productivity of the techniques, considered apart from what each technique might involve ethically, without regard to the sensible world it engenders. This is why there's no progress but capitalist progress, and why capitalism is the uninterrupted destruction of worlds. Moreover, the fact that techniques produce worlds and forms of life doesn't mean that man's essence is production, as Marx believed. So this is what technophiles and technophobes alike fail to grasp: the *ethical* nature of every technique.

It should be added that the nightmare of this epoch is not in its being the "age of technics" but in its being the age of technology. Technology is not the consummation of technical development, but on the contrary the expropriation of humans' different constitutive techniques. Technology is the *systematizing* of the most *effective* techniques, and consequently the leveling of the worlds and the relations with the world that everyone deploys. Technology is *a discourse about techniques that is constantly being projected into material reality.* Just as the ideology of the festival is the death of the real festival, and the ideology of the encounter is the actual impossibility of coming together, technology is the neutralization of all the particular techniques. In this sense capitalism is essentially technological; it is the profitable organization of the most productive techniques into a system. Its cardinal figure is not the economist but the engineer. The engineer is the specialist in techniques and thus the chief expropriator of them, one who doesn't let himself be affected by any of them, and spreads his own absence from the world everywhere he can. He's a sad and servile figure. The solidarity between capitalism and socialism is confirmed there: in the cult of the engineer. It was engineers who drew up most of the models of the neoclassical economy like pieces of contemporary trading software. Recall in this regard that Brezhnev's claim to fame was to have been an engineer in the metallurgical industry in Ukraine.

The figure of the hacker contrasts point by point with the figure of the engineer, whatever the artistic, police-directed, or entrepreneurial efforts to neutralize him may be. Whereas the engineer would capture everything that functions, in such a way that everything functions better in service to the system, the hacker asks himself "How does that work?" in order to find its flaws, but also to invent other uses, to experiment. Experimenting then means exploring what such and such a technique implies *ethically*. The hacker pulls techniques out of the technological system in order to free them. If we are slaves of technology, this is precisely because there is a whole ensemble of artifacts of our everyday existence that we take to be specifically "technical" and that we will always regard simply as black boxes of which we are the innocent users. The use of computers to attack the CIA attests rather clearly that cybernetics is no more the science of computers than astronomy is the science of telescopes. Understanding how the devices around us work, brings an immediate increase in power, giving us a purchase on what will then no longer appear as an environment, but as a world arranged in a certain way and one that we can shape. This is the hacker's perspective on the world.

These past few years, the hacker milieu has gained some sophistication politically, managing to identify friends and enemies more clearly. Several substantial obstacles stand in the way of its becoming-revolutionary, however. In 1986, "Doctor Crash" wrote: "Whether you know it or not, if you are a hacker you are a revolutionary. Don't worry, you're on the right side." It's not certain that this sort of innocence is still possible. In the hacker milieu there's an originary illusion according to which "freedom of information," "freedom of the Internet," or "freedom of the individual" can be set against those who are bent on controlling them. This is a serious misunderstanding. *Freedom and surveillance, freedom and the panopticon belong to the same paradigm of government.* Historically, the endless expansion of control procedures is the corollary of a form of power that is realized *through* the freedom of individuals. Liberal government is not one that is exercised directly on the bodies of its subjects or that expects a filial obedience from them. It's a background power, which prefers to manage space and rule over interests rather than bodies. A power that oversees, monitors, and acts minimally, intervening only where the framework is threatened, against that which *goes too far*. Only free subjects, taken en masse, are governed. Individual freedom is not something that can be brandished against the government, for it is the very mechanism on which government depends, the one it regulates as closely as possible in order to obtain, from the amalgamation of all these freedoms, the anticipated mass effect. *Ordo ab chao.* Government is that order which you obey "like eating when you're hungry and covering yourself when you're cold," that servitude which I co-produce at the same time that I pursue my happiness, that I exercise my "freedom of expression." "Market freedom requires an active and extremely vigilant politics," explained one of the founders of neoliberalism. *For the individual, monitored freedom is the only kind there is.* This is what libertarians, in their infantilism, will never understand, and it's this incomprehension that makes the libertarian idiocy attractive to some hackers. A genuinely free being is not even said to be free. It simply *is*, it exists, deploys its powers according to its being. We say of an animal that it is *en liberté*, "roaming free," only when it lives in an environment that's already completely controlled, fenced, civilized: in the park with human rules, where one indulges in a safari. "Friend" and "free" in English, and "Freund" and "frei" in German come from the same Indo-European root, which conveys the idea of a shared power that grows. Being free and having ties was one and the same thing. I am free *because I have ties*, because I am linked to a reality greater than me. In ancient Rome, the children of citizens were *liberi*: through them, it was Rome that was growing. Which goes to show how ridiculous and what a scam the individual freedom of "I do what I feel like doing" is. If they truly want to fight the government, the hackers have to give up this fetish. The cause of individual freedom is what prevents them from forming strong groups capable of laying down a real strategy, beyond a series of attacks; it's also what explains their inability to form ties beyond themselves, their incapacity for becoming a historical force. A member of Telecomix alerts his colleagues in these terms: "What is certain is that the territory you're living in is defended by persons you would do well to meet. Because they're changing the world and they won't wait for you."

Another obstacle for the hacker movement, as every new meeting of the Chaos Computer Club demonstrates, is in managing to draw a front line in its own ranks between those working for a better government, or even *the* government, and those working for its destitution. The time has come for *taking sides*. It's this basic question that Julian Assange dodges when he says: "We high-tech workers are a class and it's time we recognize ourselves as such." France has recently exploited the defect to the point of opening a university for molding "ethical hackers." Under DCRI supervision, it will train people to fight against the real hackers, those who haven't abandoned the *hacker ethic*.

These two problems merged in a case that strongly affected us. After so many attacks that so many of us applauded, Anonymous/LulzSec hackers found themselves, like Jeremy Hammond, nearly alone facing repression upon getting arrested. On Christmas day, 2011, LulzSec defaced the site of Strafor, a "private intelligence" multinational. By way of a homepage, there was now the scrolling text of *The Coming Insurrection* in English, and $700,000 was transferred from the accounts of Stratfor customers to a set of charitable associations—a Christmas present. And we weren't able to do anything, either before or after their arrest. Of course, it's safer to operate alone or in a small group—which obviously won't protect you from infiltrators—when one goes after such targets, but it's disastrous for attacks that are so political, and so clearly within the purview of global action by our party, to be reduced by the police to some private crime, punishable by decades of prison or used as a lever for pressuring this or that "Internet pirate" to turn into a government snitch.

Istanbul, June 2013.

5

LET'S DISAPPEAR

1. *A Strange Defeat.* 2. *Pacifists and Radicals—An Infernal Couple.* 3. *Government as Counter-Insurgency.* 4. *Ontological Asymmetry and Happiness.*

1. Anyone who lived through the days of December 2008 in Athens knows what the word "insurrection" signifies in a Western metropolis. The banks were in pieces, the police stations under siege, the city in the hands of the assailants. In the luxury shops, they were no longer repairing the windows, which would need to be done every morning. Nothing that embodied the police reign of normality was untouched by this wave of fire and stones whose bearers were everywhere and representatives nowhere—even the Syntagma Christmas tree was torched. At a certain point the forces of order withdrew, after running out of tear-gas grenades. Impossible to say who took over the

streets then. They say it was the "600 euros generation," the "high schoolers," the "anarchists," the
"riffraff" from the Albanian immigration, they'll
say anything. As usual, the press blamed the
"koukoulofori," the "hooded ones." The truth is
that the anarchists were overrun by this faceless
outpouring of rage. Their monopoly on wild,
masked action, inspired tags, and even Molotov
cocktails had been taken from them unceremo-
niously. The general uprising they no longer dared
to imagine was there, but it didn't resemble the
idea of it they had in their minds. An unknown
entity, an *egregore*, had been born, a spirit that
wouldn't be appeased till everything was reduced
to cinders that deserved to be. Time was on fire.
The present was fractured as payment for all the
future that had been stolen from us.

The years that followed in Greece taught us the
meaning of the word "counter-insurgency" in a
Western country. Once the wave had passed, the
hundreds of groups that had formed in the country, down to the smallest villages, tried to stay
faithful to the breach which the month of
December had opened. At one spot, people might
empty the cash registers of a supermarket, then
film themselves burning the loot. At another, an
embassy might be attacked in broad daylight in
solidarity with some friend hounded by the police
in his or her country. Some resolved, as in Italy

of the 1970s, to carry the attack to a higher level and target, using bombs or firearms, the Athens stock exchange, cops, ministries or perhaps the Microsoft headquarters. As in the 1970s, the left passed new "antiterrorist" laws. The raids, arrests, and trials multiplied. For a time, one was reduced to militating against "repression." The European Union, the World Bank, the IMF, in agreement with the Socialist government, undertook to *make Greece pay* for the unpardonable revolt. One should never underestimate the resentment of the wealthy towards the insolence of the poor. They decided to bring the whole country to heel through a string of "economic measures" more or less as violent, although spread over time, as the revolt.

This was met by dozens of general strikes called by the unions. Workers occupied ministries; inhabitants took possession of city halls; university departments and hospitals that had been "sacrificed" decided to self-organize. There was the "movement of the squares." May 10, 2010, five hundred thousand of us flooded into the center of Athens. There were several attempts to burn the Parliament. February 12, 2012, an umpteenth general strike was staged in desperate opposition to the umpteenth austerity plan. That Sunday, all of Greece, its retirees, its anarchists, its civil servants, its workers and its homeless demonstrated in a state of near-insurrection. With downtown Athens again in flames, that evening was a paroxysm of jubilation and weariness: the movement perceived all its power, but also realized it didn't know what to do with it. Over the years, in spite of thousands of direct actions, hundreds of occupations, millions of Greeks in the streets, the euphoria of rebellion was dampened in the damper of "crisis." The embers stayed active under the ashes, certainly. The movement found other forms, providing itself with cooperatives, social centers, "networks of exchange without middlemen," and even self-managed factories and health clinics. It became more "constructive" in a sense. The fact remains that we were defeated, that one the biggest offensives of our party during the past few decades was driven back through debt impositions, exaggerated prison sentences, and generalized bankruptcy. The free used clothing won't make Greeks forget the counter-insurgency's determination to plunge them up to their necks in privation. Power may have tottered and given the momentary impression of disap-pearing, but it was able to shift the terrain of confrontation and catch the movement off balance. The Greeks were blackmailed by this alternative: "government or chaos." What they got was govern-ment *and* chaos—plus immiseration as a bonus.

With its anarchist movement stronger than anywhere else, with its people largely uneasy with the very fact of being governed, with its always-already failed state, Greece stands as a textbook case of our defeated insurrections. Jacking the police, smashing the banks and temporarily routing a government is still not destituting it all. What the Greek case shows us is that without a concrete idea of what a victory would be, we can't help but be defeated. Insurrectionary determination is not enough; our confusion is still too thick. Hopefully, studying our defeats will serve at least to dispel it somewhat.

2. Forty years of triumphant counterrevolution in the West have inflicted two matching weaknesses on us: pacifism and radicalism. They're both harmful, but in combination they form a ruthless apparatus.

Pacifism lies, and lies to itself, by making public discussion and general assembly the be-all and end-all of political practice. That explains why the squares movement, for example, was incapable of becoming anything more than a terminal starting point. To grasp what the political means, there seems to be no choice but to take another detour through Greece, but ancient Greece this time. After all, the political was invented there. Pacifists are reluctant to remember this, but early on, the ancient Greeks invented democracy as a continuation of war by other means. The assembly practice on the scale of the city-state came directly from the assembly of warriors. Equality of speech stemmed from equality in the face of death. Athenian democracy was a hoplitic democracy. One was a citizen *because one was a soldier*—hence the exclusion of women and slaves. In a culture as violently agonistic as classical Greek culture, debate itself was understood as a moment of warlike confrontation, between citizens this time, in the sphere of speech, with the arms of persuasion. Moreover, "agon" signifies "assembly" as much as "competition." The complete Greek citizen was one who was victorious both with arms and with discourse.

Above all, the ancient Greeks conceived assembly democracy in combination with *warfare as organized carnage*, and the former as the guarantor of the latter. It's significant that the Greeks are credited with the invention of democracy only on condition that its link with that rather exceptional type of massacre based on the phalanx is glossed over—that is, with the invention of a form of line warfare that replaces skill, bravery, prowess, extraordinary strength, and genius with pure and simple discipline, absolute submission of each to the whole. When the Persians found themselves facing such an *effective* way of waging war, but one that reduced the life of the foot soldier in the phalanx to nothing, they rightly judged it to be perfectly barbaric, as did so many of those enemies whom the Western armies were to crush subsequently. The Athenian farmer getting himself heroically slaughtered in the front rank of the phalanx in view of his friends and relatives was thus the flip side of the active citizen taking part in the *Boule*. The lifeless arms of the corpses strewn over the ancient battlefield were the necessary counterparts of the arms raised to intervene in the deliberations of the assembly. This Greek model of warfare is so firmly entrenched in the Western imaginary it's almost forgotten that at the very time when the hoplites were awarding the victory to that phalanx of the two that would accept the maximun number of deaths in the decisive clash rather than yield ground, the Chinese were inventing an art of war that consisted precisely in minimizing losses and avoiding battle as much as possible, in trying to "win the battle before the battle"—even if this also meant exterminating the defeated army once the victory was obtained. The equation "war=armed confrontation=carnage" extended from ancient Greece down through the 20th century. It's basically been the aberrant Western definition of warfare for two thousand five hundred years. The fact that "irregular warfare," "psychological warfare," "little war" or "guerilla" are the names given to what is elsewhere *the norm of warfare* is only one aspect of that particular aberration.

The sincere pacifist, one who is not simply rationalizing his own cowardice, performs the feat of being doubly mistaken about the nature of the phenomenon he claims to be combating. Not only is war not reducible to armed confrontation or carnage, it is the very matrix of the assembly politics that the pacifist advocates. "A real warrior," said Sun Tzu, "is not bellicose. A real fighter is not violent. A victor avoids combat." Two world conflicts and a terrifying planetary fight against "terrorism" have shown us that the bloodiest campaigns of extermination are conducted in the name of peace. At bottom, the rejection of war only expresses an infantile or senile refusal to recognize the existence of otherness. War is not carnage, but the logic that regulates the contact of heterogeneous powers. It is waged everywhere, in countless forms, and more often than not by peaceful means. If there's a multiplicity of worlds, if there's an irreducible plurality of forms of life, then war is the law of their co-existence on this earth. For nothing allows us to foresee the outcome of their encounter: contraries don't dwell in separate worlds. If we are not unified individuals endowed with a definitive identity as the social policing of roles would have it, but the locus of a conflictual play of forces whose successive configurations only form temporary equilibriums, we have to recognize that war is in us—holy war, as René Daumal called it. Peace is neither possible nor desirable. Conflict is the very stuff of what exists. So the thing to do is to acquire an art of conducting it, which is an art of living on a situational footing, and which requires a finesse and an existential mobility instead of a readiness to crush whatever is not us.

Pacifism attests therefore either to a deep stupidity or a complete lack of good faith. Even our immune system depends on the distinction between friend and enemy, without which we would die of cancer or some other autoimmune disease. Actually, we do die of cancers and autoimmune diseases. The tactical refusal of confrontation is itself only a stratagem of warfare. It's easy to understand, for example, why the Oaxaca Commune immediately declared itself peaceful. It wasn't a matter of refuting war, but of refusing to be defeated in a confrontation with the Mexican state and its henchmen. As some Cairo comrades explained it, "One mustn't mistake the tactic we employ when we chant 'nonviolence' for a fetishizing of non-violence." It's amazing, furthermore, how much historical falsification it takes to find forebears who are presentable to pacifism! Think of poor Thoreau who was barely deceased when they made him into a theoretician of *Civil Disobedience*, by amputating the title of his text, *Resistance to Civil Government*. This was the man who wrote in longhand in his *Plea for Captain John Brown*: "I think that for once the Sharpe's rifles and the revolvers were employed in a righteous cause. The tools were in the hands of one who could use them. The same indignation that is said to have cleared the temple once will clear it again. The question is not about the weapon, but the spirit in which you use it." But the most farcical case of false genealogy has to be the way Nelson Mandela, the founder of the armed-struggle organization of the ANC, was turned into a global icon of peace. He lays it out himself: "I said that the time for passive resistance had ended, that nonviolence was a useless strategy and could never overturn a white minority regime bent on retaining its power at any cost. At the end of the day, I said, violence was the only weapon that would destroy apartheid and we must be prepared, in the near future, to use that weapon. The crowd was excited; the youth in particular were clapping and cheering. They were ready to act on what I said right then and there. At that point I began to sing a freedom song, the lyrics of which say, 'There are the enemies, let us take our weapons and attack them.' I sang this song and the crowd joined in, and when the song was finished, I pointed to the police and said, 'There, there are our enemies!'"

Decades of pacification of the masses and massification of fears have made pacifism the spontaneous political consciousness of the *citizen*. With every movement that develops now one has to grapple with this awful state of affairs. One can cite the pacifists delivering black-clad rioters over to the police at the Plaça Catalunya in 2011, or the harassment and verbal lynching of "Black Bloc" protesters by the same in Genoa in 2001. In response to that, the revolutionary milieus secreted, as a kind of antibody, the figure of the radical— someone who always takes the opposing view to the citizen. To the moral proscription of violence by the one, the other always replies with his purely ideological apology of violence. Where the pacifist always seeks to absolve himself of the state of the world, to remain good by doing no evil, the radical seeks to absolve himself of participation in the "existing state of things" through minor illegalities embellished with hardcore "position statements." Both aspire to purity, one through violent action, the other by abstaining from it. Each is the other's nightmare. It's not certain that these two figures would go on existing for long if each one didn't have the other deep inside him. As if the radical only lived to make the pacifist shudder inside, and vice versa. It's fitting that the bible of American citizen struggles since the 1970s is titled *Rules for Radicals*—by Saul Alinsky. Because pacifists and radicals are joined together in the same refusal of the world. They take pleasure in their disjunction from every situation. It gets them high, makes them feel like they're in touch with some sort of excellence. They prefer living as extraterrestrials— such is the comfort that is authorized, for a

while still, by life in the metropolis, their privileged biotope.

Since the catastrophic defeat of the 1970s, the
moral question of radicality has gradually replaced
the *strategic* question of revolution. That is, revolution
has suffered the same fate as everything else in those
decades: it has been privatized. It has become an
opportunity for personal validation, with radicality as
the standard of evaluation. "Revolutionary" acts are
no longer appraised in terms of the situation in
which they are embedded, the possibilities they
open up or close. What happens instead is that a
form is extracted from each one of them. A particular
sabotage, occurring at a particular moment, for a
particular reason, becomes simply *a* sabotage. And
the sabotage quietly takes its place among certified
revolutionary practices on a scale where throwing a
Molotov cocktail ranks higher than throwing rocks,
but lower than kneecapping, which itself is not
worth as much as a bomb. The problem is that no
form of action is revolutionary in itself: sabotage has
also been practiced by reformists and by Nazis. A
movement's degree of "violence" is not indicative of
its revolutionary determination. The "radicality" of
a demonstration isn't measured by the number of
shop windows broken. Or if it is, then the "radicality" criterion should be left to those in the habit
of *measuring* political phenomena and ranking them
on their skeletal moral scale.

Anyone who begins to frequent radical milieus is immediately struck by the gap between their discourse and their practice, between their ambitions and their isolation. It seems as if they were dedicated to a kind of constant self-incapacitation. One soon understands that they're not engaged in constructing a real revolutionary force, but in a quest for radicality that is sufficient in itself—and is played out equally well on the terrain of direct action, feminism or ecology. The petty terror that reigns there and makes everyone so *stiff* is not that of the Bolshevik Party. It's more like that of fashion, that terror which no one exerts in person, but which affects everyone alike. In these milieus, one is afraid of not being radical anymore, just as elsewhere one fears not being fashionable, cool or hip. It doesn't take much to spoil a reputation. One avoids going to the root of things in favor of a superficial consumption of theories, demos, and relations. The fierce competition between groups and inside them causes them to periodically implode. But there's always fresh, young, and abused flesh to make up for the departure of the exhausted, the damaged, the disgusted, and the *emptied-out*. An a posteriori bewilderment overtakes the person who's deserted these circles: how can anyone submit to such a mutilating pressure for such enigmatic stakes? It's approximately the same kind of bewilderment that must take hold of any overworked ex-manager turned baker when he looks back on his previous life. The isolation of these milieus is structural: between them and the world they've interposed radicality as a standard. They don't perceive phenomena anymore, just their measure. At a certain point in the autophagy, some will compete for most radical *by critiquing the milieu itself*, which won't make the slightest dent in its structure. "It seems to us that what really reduces our freedom," wrote Malatesta, "and makes intiative impossible, is disempowering isolation." This being the case, that a fraction of the anarchists declare themselves "nihilists" is only logical: nihilism is the incapacity to believe in what one does believe in—in our context, revolution. Besides, there are no nihilists, there are only powerless individuals.

The radical defining himself as a producer of actions and discourses has ended up fabricating a purely quantitative idea of revolution—as a kind of crisis of overproduction of acts of individual revolt. "Let's not lose sight of the fact," wrote Émile Henry back then already, "that revolution will simply be the resultant of all these particular revolts." History is there to contradict that notion: whether it's the French, Russian, or Tunisian revolution, in every instance revolution results from the shock encounter between a particular act—the storming of a prison, a military defeat, the suicide of a mobile fruit vendor—and the general situation, and not the arithmetical addition of separate acts of revolt. Meanwhile, that absurd definition of revolution is doing its foreseeable damage: one wears oneself out in an activism that leads nowhere, one devotes oneself to a dreadful cult of performance where it's a matter of actualizing one's radical identity at every moment, here and now—in a demo, in love, or in discourse. This lasts for a time—the time of a *burnout*, depression, or repression. And one hasn't changed anything.

An accumulation of gestures is not enough to make up a strategy because there is no gesture in the absolute. A gesture is revolutionary not by its own content but by the sequence of effects it engenders. The situation is what determines the meaning of the act, not the intention of its authors. Sun Tzu said that "victory must be demanded of the situation." Every situation is composite, traversed by lines of force, tensions, explicit or latent conflicts. Engaging with the war that *is present*, acting strategically, requires that we start from an openness to the situation, that we understand its inner dynamic, the relations of force that configure it, the polarities that give it its dynamism. An action is revolutionary or not depending on the meaning it acquires from contact with the world. Throwing a rock is never just "rock-throwing." It can freeze a situation or touch off an intifada. The idea that a struggle can be "radicalized" by injecting a whole passel of allegedly radical practices and discourses into it is the politics of an extraterrestrial. A movement lives only through a series of shifts that it effects over time. So at every moment there is a certain distance between its present state and its potential. If it stops developing, if it leaves its potential unrealized, it dies. A decisive act is one that is a notch ahead of the movement's state, and which, breaking with the status quo, gives it access to its own potential. This act can be that of occupying, smashing, attacking, or simply speaking truthfully. The state of the movement is what decides. *A thing is revolutionary that actually causes revolutions.* While this can only be determined after the event, a certain sensitivity to the situation plus a dose of historical knowledge helps one intuit the matter.

Let's leave the radicality worry to the depressives, the Young-Girls, and the losers, then. The real question for revolutionaries is how to make the lively powers in which one participates increase, how to nurture the *revolutionizing* developments so as to arrive finally at a revolutionary *situation.* All those who draw satisfaction from dogmatically contrasting "radicals" with "citizens," "active rebels" with the passive population, place obstacles in the path of such developments. On this point, they anticipate the work of the police. In the current period, *tact* should be considered the cardinal revolutionary virtue, and not abstract radicality—and by "tact" we mean the art of nurturing revolutionary becomings.

Among the miracles of the Susa Valley struggle, one has to include the way it succeeded in tearing a good number of radicals away from their painfully constructed identity. It brought them back down to earth. In contact again with a real situation, they were able to shed most of their ideological spacesuit—not without incurring the inexhaustible resentment of those still confined in their interstellar radicality where breathing is such a problem. Undoubtedly, the happy outcome was due to this struggle's special art of avoiding capture in the image that power holds out to it—whether it's that of an ecology movement of legalistic citizens or that of an armed-violence vanguard. Alternating family-style demonstrations with attacks on the TAV construction site, resorting to sabotage at one moment and partnership with the valley's mayors the next, associating anarchists and Catholic grandmas, this struggle is revolutionary at least insofar as it has been able to deactivate the infernal coupling of pacifism and radicalism. "Living in a political manner," reflected a Stalinist dandy shortly before dying, "means acting instead of being acted upon, it means doing politics instead of being done by it, remade by it. It's to engage in combat, a series of combats, to wage war, one's own war with war objectives, immediate and longterm perspectives, a strategy, a tactic."

3. "Civil war," said Foucault, "is the matrix of all the power struggles, of all the power strategies and, consequently, the matrix of all the struggles over and against power." He added, "civil war not only brings collective elements into play, but it constitutes them. Far from being the process through which one comes down again from the republic to individuality, from the sovereign to the state of nature, from the collective order to the war of all against all, civil war is the process through and by which a certain number of new collectivities that had not seen the light of day constitute themselves." It's on this plane of perception that basically every political existence deploys. Pacifism that has already lost and radicalism that only intends to lose are two ways of not seeing this. Of not seeing that war is not essentially military in nature. That life is essentially strategic. The irony of our epoch has it that the only ones who situate war where it is conducted, and thus reveal the plane where all government operates, happen to be the counter-revolutionaries themselves. It is striking to note that in the last half-century the non-militaries began rejecting war in all its forms, and at the very

time when the militaries were developing a non-military concept, a *civil concept of war.*

A few examples, casually excerpted from contemporary articles:

The locus of collective armed conflict has gradually expanded the battlefield to include the whole earth. In like manner, its duration may now be indefinite, without there being a declaration of war or any armistice [...] For this reason contemporary strategists emphasize that modern victory results from conquering the hearts of the members of a population rather than their territory. Submission must be gained through adherence and adherence through esteem. Indeed, it's a matter of imposing one's purpose on the inner individual, where the social contact between human collectivities is established at present. Stripped bare by world homogenization, contacted by globalisation, and penetrated by telecommunication, henceforth the front will be situated in the inner being of each of the members that make up the collectivities. [...] This sort of fabrication of passive partisans can be summed up by the catchphrase: "The front within every person, and no one on any front." [...] The whole politico-strategic challenge of a world that is neither at war or at peace, which precludes all settlement of conflict by means of the classic military juridical voices, consists in preventing passive partisans on the verge of action, at the threshold of belligerence, from becoming active partisans. (Laurent Danet, "*La polémosphère*")

At present, given that the terrain of warfare has extended beyond the ground, sea, space, and electronic fields into those of society, politics, economics, diplomacy, culture, and even psychology, the interaction among the different factors makes it very difficult to maintain the preponderance of the military domain as the dominant one in every war. The idea that war can unfold in unwarlike domains is foreign to reason and hard to accept, but events increasingly show this to be the trend. [...] In this sense, there no longer exists any area of life that cannot serve war and there are almost no areas remaining that do not present the offensive aspect of war. (Qiao Liang and Wang Xiangsui, *La guerre hors limite*)

The probable war is not waged "between" societies, but "within" societies [...] Since the objective is human society, its governance, its social contract, its institutions, and no longer this or that province, river, or border, there is no longer any line or terrain to conquer or protect. The only front that the engaged forces must hold is that of the populations. [...] To win the war is to control the milieu. [...] It's no longer a question of perceiving a mass of tanks and of pinpointing potential targets, but of understanding social milieus, behaviors, psychologies. It's a matter of influencing human intentions through a selective and appropriate application of force. [...] Military actions are truly "a manner of speaking": henceforth, every major operation is above all a communication operation whose every act, even a minor act, speaks louder than words. [...] To wage war is first and foremost to manage perceptions, those of the set of actors, whether close by or far away, direct or indirect. (General Vincent Desportes, *La guerre probable*)

The developed postmodern societies have become extremely complex and hence very fragile. To prevent their collapse in the event of a "breakdown," it's imperative that they decentralize (the salvation will come from the margins and not the institutions) [...] It will be necessary to rely on local forces (self-defense militias, paramilitary groups, private military associations), first from a practical standpoint owing to their knowledge of the milieu and the populations, second, because on the part of the State it will be a mark of confidence that federates the different initiatives and reinforces them, and last and most important, because they are more apt to find appropriate and original (unconventional) solutions to delicate situations. In other words, the response called for by unconventional warfare needs to be citizen-based and paramilitary, rather than having a police and military focus. [...] If Hezbollah has become a first-rate international actor, if the neo-Zapatista movement manages to represent an alternative to neoliberal globalization, then one has admit that the "local" can interact with the "global" and that this interaction is truly one of the major strategic characteristics of our time. [...] To put it briefly, a local-global interaction must be answered by a different interaction of the same type, supported not by the state apparatus (diplomacy, army), but by the local element par excellence—the citizen. (Bernard Wicht, *Vers l'ordre oblique: la contre-guérilla à l'âge de l'infoguerre*)

After reading that, one has a slightly different take on the role of the militias of citizen sweepers and the appeals for snitching following the riots of August 1011 in England, or the bringing in— then the opportune elimination when "the pitbull got too big"—of the Golden Dawn fascists as players in the Greek political game. To say nothing of the recent arming of citizen militias by the Mexican federal state in Michoacán. What is happening to us at present can be summed up more or less in this way: *from being a military doctrine, counter-insurgency has become a principle of government.* One of the cables of American diplomacy revealed by Wikileaks confirms this, bluntly: "The program of pacification of the favelas incorporates certain characteristics of the doctrine and strategy of counter-insurgency of the United States in Afghanistan and Iraq." The era can be reduced ultimately to this struggle, this race, between the possibility of insurrection and the partisans of counter-insurrection. Moreover, this is what the rare outburst of political chattering triggered in the West by the "Arab revolutions" served to mask. To mask, for example, the fact that cutting off all communication in the working-class areas, as Mubarak did at the start of the uprising, was not just the impulsive act of an addled dictator, but a strict application of the NATO report, *Urban Operations in the Year 2020.*

There is no world government; what there is instead is a worldwide network of local apparatuses of government, that is, a global, reticular, counterinsurgency machinery. Snowden's revelations show this amply: secret services, multinationals, and political networks collaborate shamelessly, even beyond a nation-state level that nobody cares about now. In this regard, there is no center and periphery, internal security and foreign operations. What is tried out on faraway peoples will be the fate that is in store for one's own people. The troops that massacred the Parisian proletariat in June of 1848 had honed their skills in the "street war," the raids and torchings called *enfumades* in Algeria during colonization. The Italian mountain infantry batallions, recently returned from Afghanistan, were redeployed in the Susa Valley. In the West, using the armed forces on national territory in cases of major disorder is longer even a taboo, it's a standard scenario. From health crisis to imminent terrorist attack, their minds have been methodically prepared for it. They train everywhere for urban battles, for "pacification," for "post-conflict" stabilization. They maintain their readiness for the coming insurrections.

The counter-insugency doctrines should be read, therefore, as theories of the war being waged against us, doctrines that partly define, among so many other things, our common situation in this era. They should be read both as a qualitative leap in the concept of war, short of which we cannot situate ourselves, and as a deceptive mirror. Although the doctrines of counter-insurgency warfare are patterned after the successive revolutionary doctrines, one cannot negatively deduce any theory of insurrection from counter-insurgency theories. That is the logical trap. It no longer suffices for us to wage the "little war," to attack by surprise, to deprive the adversary of any target. Even that kind of asymmetry has been diminished. As far as war and strategy are concerned, it's not enough to catch up: we have to move into the lead. We need a strategy that's aimed not at the adversary but at his strategy, that turns it back against itself, making it so that the more he thinks he's winning the more surely he's heading towards his defeat.

The fact that counter-insurgency has made society itself its theater of operations doesn't at all indicate that the war to be waged is the "social war" that some anarchists mouth off about. The main defect of this notion is that by lumping the offensives carried out by "the State and Capital" and those of their adversaries under the same rubric, it places subversives in a relation of symmetrical warfare. The smashed window of an Air France office in retaliation for the expulsion of undocumented migrants is declared to be an "act of social war," on a par with a wave of arrests targeting people fighting against detention centers. While we have to recognize an undeniable determination on the part of many upholders of "social war," they accept fighting the state head-to-head, on a terrain that has always belonged to it and no one else. Only the forces involved in this case are dissymmetrical. A crushing defeat is inevitable.

The idea of social war is actually just an unsuccessful updating of "class war," maintaining that each one's position in the relations of production no longer has the formal clarity of the Fordist factory. It sometimes seems as if revolutionaries are compelled to constitute themselves on the same model as what they're fighting. Thus, as a member of the International Workingmen's Association summarized it in 1871, the bosses being organized worldwide around their interests as a class, the proletariat must likewise organize itself worldwide, as a working class and around its interests. As a member of the young Bolshevik Party explained it, the tsarist regime was organized into a disciplined and hierarchical politico-military machine, so the Party should also organize itself into a disciplined and hierarchical politico-military machine. One can multiply the historical cases, all equally tragic, of this *curse of symmetry.* Take the Algerian FLN, which in its methods came to closely resemble the colonial occupiers well before its victory. Or the Red Brigades, who imagined that by taking out the fifty men who were thought to constitute the "core of the State" they would be able to appropriate the whole machine. Today, the most wrongheaded expression of this tragedy of symmetry comes out of the doddering mouths of the new left. What they say is that set against the diffuse Empire, which is structured into a network, but endowed with command centers all the same, there are the multitudes, just as diffuse, structured into a network, but endowed nonetheless with a bureaucracy capable of occupying the command centers when the day comes.

Marked by this kind of symmetry, revolt is bound to fail—not only because it presents an easy target, a *recognizable* face, but above all because it eventually takes on the features of its adversary. To be convinced of this, open *Counterinsurgency Warfare: Theory and Practice*, by David Galula, for example. One finds therein, methodically laid out in detail, the steps to a definitive victory of a loyalist force over generic insurgents. "The best cause for the insurgent is one that, by definition, can attract the largest number of supporters and repel the minimum of opponents [...] It is not absolutely necessary that the problem be acute, although the insurgent's work is facilitated if such is the case. If the problem is merely latent, the first task of the insurgent is to make it acute by 'raising the political consciousness of the masses' […] The insurgent is not restricted to the choice of a single cause. Unless he has found an overall cause, like anti-colonialism, which is sufficient in itself because it combines all the political, social, economic, racial, religious, and cultural causes […], he has much to gain by selecting an assortment of causes especially tailored for the various groups in the society that he is seeking to take over."

Who is Galula's "insurgent"? None other than the distorted reflection of the Western politician, official, or publicist: cynical, external to every situation, devoid of any genuine desire, except for an outsize hunger for control. The insurgent that Galula knows how to combat is a stranger to the world just as he's a stranger to any belief. For that officer, Galula, insurrection never emanates from the population, which only aspires to security, basically, and tends to go with the party that protects it the best or threatens it the least. The population is only a pawn, an inert mass, a *marsh*, in the struggle between several elites. It can seem astonishing that power's notion of the insurgent wavers between the figure of the fanatic and that of the crafty lobbyist—but this is less surprising than the eagerness of so many revolutionaries to put on those unpleasant masks. Always this same symmetrical understanding of warfare, even the "asymmetrical" kind—groupuscules competing for control of the population, and always maintaining an outsider's relation with it. In the end, this is the monumental error of counter-insurgency: despite its success absorbing the asymmetry introduced by guerilla tactics, it still continues to produce the figure of the "terrorist" *based on what it is itself.* And this is to our advantage, then, provided we don't allow ourselves to embody that figure. It's what all effective revolutionary strategy must accept as its point of departure. The failure of the American strategy in Iraq and Afghanistan bears witness. Counter-insurgency did such a good job of turning "the population" around that the Obama administration has to routinely and surgically assassinate, via drone, anything that might resemble an insurgent.

4. If the insurgents' war against the government needs to be asymmetrical, it's because there is an *ontological* asymmetry between them, and hence a disagreement about the very definition of war, about its methods as well as its objectives. We other revolutionaries are both the focus and the target of the permanent offensive that government has become. We *are* the "hearts and minds" that must be conquered. We *are* the "crowds" that are to be controlled. We *are* the environment in which the governmental agents evolve and which they mean to subdue, and not a rival entity in the race for power. We don't fight in the midst of the people "like fish in water"; we're the water itself, in which our enemies flounder—soluble fish. We don't hide in ambush among the plebs of this world, because it's also within us that the plebs hide. The vitality and the plundering, the rage and the craftiness, the truth and the subterfuge all spring from deep within us. There is *no one* to be organized. We are that material which grows from within, which organizes itself and develops itself. The true asymmetry lies there, and our real position of strength is there. Those who make their belief into an article of export, through terror or performance, instead of dealing with what exists where they are, only cut themselves off from themselves and their base. It's not a matter of snatching the "support of the population," nor even its indulgent passivity, from the enemy: we must make it so *there is no longer a population.* The population has never been the *object* of government without first being its *product.* It ceases to exist once it ceases to be governable. This is what's involved in the muffled battle that rages after every uprising: dissolving the power that had formed, focused, and deployed in that event. Governing has never been anything but denying the people all political capacity, that is, preventing insurrection.

Separating those governed from their political power to act is what the police are about whenever they try to "isolate the violent ones" at the end of a righteous demonstration. Nothing is more effective for crushing an insurrection than causing a split within the insurgent mass between an innocent or vaguely consenting population and its vanguard, who are militarized, hence minoritarian, usually clandestine, and soon to be "terrorist." We owe the most complete example of such a tactic to Frank Kitson, the godfather of British counter-insurgency. In the years following the extraordinary conflict that engulfed Northern Ireland in August 1969, the great strength of the IRA was to stand together with the Catholic districts that had declared themselves autonomous and called for its assistance, at Belfast and Derry, during the riots. Free Derry, Short Strand, Ardoyne: three of those no-go areas that one finds so often in apartheid territories, and still encircled today by kilometers of "peace lines." The ghettoes had risen up, barricading their entry points and closing them to the cops and the loyalists. Fifteen-year-old kids alternated mornings at school with nights on the barricades. The most repectable members of the community did the shopping for ten and organized clandestine grocery outlets for those who couldn't safely go out on their own. Although caught unprepared by the summer's events, the Provisional IRA blended into the extremely dense ethical fabric of those enclaves that were in a constant state of insurrection. From that position of irreducible strength, everything seemed possible. The year 1972 would be the year of victory.

Somewhat taken aback, the counter-insurgency went all out. At the end of a military operation with no equivalent for Great Britain since the Suez crisis, the districts were emptied out, the enclaves were broken, in this way effectively separating the "professional" revolutionaries from the riotous populations that risen up in 1969, tearing them away from the thousand complicities that had been woven. Through this maneuver, the Provisional IRA was constrained to being nothing more than an armed faction, a paramilitary group, impressive and determined to be sure, but headed toward exhaustion, internment without trial, and summary executions. The tactic of repression seems to have consisted in *bringing a radical revolutionary subject into existence*, and separating it from everything that made it a vital force of the Catholic community: a territorial anchorage, an everyday life, a youthfulness. And as if that wasn't enough, false IRA attacks were organized to finish turning a paralyzed population against it. From counter gangs to false flag operations, nothing was ruled out for making the IRA into a clandestine monster, territorially and politically detached from what constituted the strength of the republican movement: the districts, their sense of making-do and of organization, their custom of rioting. Once the "paramilitaries" were isolated, and the thousand exceptional procedures for annihilating them were routinized, it was just a matter of waiting for the "troubles" to dissipate of their own accord.

When the most indiscriminate repression comes down on us, we should be careful, then, not to see it as the conclusive proof of our radicality. We shouldn't think they are out to *destroy* us. We should start rather from the hypothesis that they're out to *produce* us. Produce us as a political subject, as "anarchists," as "Black Bloc," as "anti-system" radicals, to extract us from the generic population by assigning us a political identity. When repression strikes us, let's begin *by not taking ourselves for ourselves.* Let's dissolve the fantastical terrorist subject which the counter-insurgency theorists take such pains to impersonate, a subject the representation of which serves mainly to produce the "population" as a foil—the population as an apathetic and apolitical heap, an immature mass just good enough for being governed, for having its hunger pangs and consumer dreams satisfied.

Revolutionaries have no call to convert the "population" from the bogus exteriority of who knows what "social project." They should start instead from their own presence, from the places they inhabit, the territories they're familiar with, the ties that link them to what is going on around them. Identification of the enemy and effective strategies and tactics are things that come from living and not from any prior declaration of belief. *The logic of increasing power is all that can be set against that of taking power.* Fully inhabiting is all that can be set against the paradigm of government. One can throw oneself onto the state apparatus, but if the terrain that's won is not immediately filled with a new life, government will end up taking it back. Raúl Zibechi writes this about the Aymara insurrection in Bolivia in 2003: "Actions of this magnitude cannot be carried out successfully without the existence of a dense network of relationships between persons—relationships that are also forms of organization. The problem is that we are unwilling to consider that in everyday life the relationships between neighbors, between friends, between comrades, or between family, are as important as those of the union, the party, or even the state itself. [...] Established relationships, codified through formal agreements, are often more important in Western culture than those loyalties woven by informal ties." We need to give the same care to the smallest everyday details of our shared life as we give to the revolution. For insurrection is the displacement of this organization that is not one—not being detachable from ordinary life—onto an offensive terrain. It is a qualitative leap in the ethical dimension, not a break with the everyday, finally consummated. Zibechi goes on to say: "The same bodies that sustain everyday life sustain the uprising (the neighborhood assemblies in the local councils of El Alto). The rotation of tasks and the obligatory character that regulates everyday community life, also regulates the task of blocking roads and streets." In this way the sterile distinction between spontaneity and organization is dissolved. There's not on one hand a prepolitical, unreflected, "spontaneous" sphere of existence and on the other a political, rational, organized sphere. Those with shitty relationships can only have a shitty politics.

This doesn't mean that in order to conduct a winning offensive we must ban any inclination to conflict among us—conflict, not double dealing and scheming. It's largely because the Palestinian resistance has never prevented differences from existing within it—even at the cost of open confrontations—that it has been able to give the Israeli army a hard time. Here as elsewhere, political fragmentation is just as much the sign of an undeniable ethical vitality as it is the nightmare of the intelligence agencies charged with mapping, then annihilating, resistance. An Israeli architect writes as follows: "The Israeli and Palestinian methods of fighting are fundamentally different. The fractured Palestinian resistance is composed of a multiplicity of organizations, each having a more or less independent armed wing—Iz Adin al-Qassam for Hamas, Saraya al Quds (the Jerusalem Brigades) for Islamic Jihad, Al-Aqsa Martyrs Brigade, Force 17 and Tanzim al-Fatah for Fatah. These are supplemented by the independent PRC (Popular Resistance Committees) and imagined or real members of Hizbollah and/or Al-Qaeda. The fact that these organizations shift between cooperation, competition, and violent conflict increases the general complexity of their interactions and with it their collective capacity, efficiency, and resilience. The diffuse nature of Palestinian resistance and the fact that knowledge, skills, and munitions are transferred within and between these organizations—and that they sometimes stage joint attacks and at others compete to outdo each other—substantially reduces the effect that the Israeli occupation forces seek to achieve by attacking them." Accommodating internal conflict when it presents itself honestly, doesn't interfere at all with the concrete elaboration of an insurrectionary strategy. On the contrary, it's the best way for a movement to stay vital, to keep the essential questions open, to make the necessary shifts in a timely manner. But if we accept civil war, *including in our midst*, it's not only because in itself this constitutes a good strategy for defeating imperial offensives. It's also and above all because it accords with the idea we have of life. Indeed, if being revolutionary implies an attachment to certain truths, it follows from the irreducible plurality of the latter that our party will never enjoy a peaceful unity. As far as organization is concerned, then, there will be no choosing between fraternal peace and fratricidal war. We will need to choose between the forms of internal confrontations that strengthen revolutions and those that hinder them.

To the question, "your idea of happiness?" Marx replied, "to fight." To the question, "why do you fight?" we reply that our idea of happiness requires it.

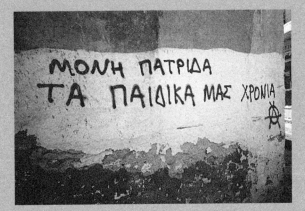

Crete, 2008.

6

OUR ONLY HOMELAND: CHILDHOOD

1. *There Is No "Society" to Be Defended or Destroyed.* 2. *Selection Needs to Be Turned into Secession.* 3. *There Are No "Local Struggles," but a War of Worlds.*

1. On May 5, 2010, Athens is experiencing one of those days of general strike where everyone is in the streets. The atmosphere is springlike and combative. Trade unionists, Maoists, anarchists, civil servants and pensioners, young people and immigrants, the city center is literally flooded with demonstrators. The country has discovered the incredible memorandums of the Troika and reacted with a rage that's still intact. Parliament, which is in the process of passing a new set of "austerity" measures, has come within an inch of being stormed. Failing that, it's the Ministry of Economics that yields and begins to burn. Pretty

much everywhere on the routes, cobblestones are wedged out, banks are smashed, there are confrontations with the police, who are generous with their flashbangs and horrible tear gas canisters imported from Israel. The anarchists ritually launch their Molotov cocktails and, less customary, are applauded by the crowd. People chant the classic "cops, pigs, killers" and some shout "burn down the parliament!" "Government kills!" What resembles the beginning of an uprising will come to a halt in early afternoon, brought down in full flight by a government bulletin. It seems that anarchists, after having tried to light up the Ianos bookstore on Stadiou Street, set fire to a bank that had not respected the general strike proclamation. There were employees inside. Three of them died of suffocation, one of them a pregnant woman. It was not immediately specified that the management had locked the one emergency exit. The Marfin Bank event stunned and deflated the anarchist movement. The movement, and not the government, found itself in the role of killer. Under the pressure of the event, the rift between "social anarchists" and "nihilist anarchists" that had been growing since December 2008 reached its maximum intensity. There was a re-emergence of the old question of whether to engage with society in order to change it, suggesting and offering it examples of other forms of organization, or to set about simply destroying it, without sparing those who, through their passivity and submission, ensured its perpetuation. People got into a worse muddle than ever on this point. It went beyond diatribes. Blood was shed in the fighting that took place, to the great amusement of the police.

The tragic aspect of this affair, perhaps, is that people tore each other apart around a question that is no longer relevant, which would explain why the debate has remained so sterile. Perhaps there is no longer a "society" to destroy or persuade. Perhaps that fiction which was born at the end of the 17th century and which occupied so many revolutionaries and rulers for two centuries has breathed its last without our realizing it. But we would still need to know how to mourn its passing, since we're immune to the nostalgia of the sociologist who laments *The End of Societies* as well as to the neoliberal opportunism that declared one day with martial aplomb: "there is no such thing as society."

In the 17th century, "civil society" was what stood in contrast to the "state of nature." It was the fact of being "joined together under the same government and the same laws." "Society" was a certain state of civilization, or it was "the good aristocratic society," one that excluded the multitude of commoners. In the course of the 18th century, as liberal governmentality developed along with the "dismal science" corresponding to it, "political economy," "civil society" came to denote bourgeois society. It no longer stood in contrast to the state of nature, it became "natural" as it were, as the habit spread of considering it natural for man to behave as an economic creature. So "civil society" was now understood as the entity that was counterposed to the State. It would take all the Saint-Simonism, all the scientism, all the socialism, all the positivism, and all the colonialism of the 19th century to impose the self-evidence of society, the self-evidence that, in all the manifestations of their existence, humans form a great family, a species totality. At the end of the 19th century, *everything became "social"*: housing, the question, economy, reform, sciences, hygiene, security, labor, and even war—social war. In 1894, at the height of this movement, a group of concerned philanthropists even established a "Social Museum" in Paris with the mission of testing and disseminating techniques for improving, pacifying, and sanitizing "social life." In the 18th century, no one would have dreamed of founding a "science" like "sociology," much less doing so on the model of biology.

At bottom, "society" only denotes the projected shadow of the successive modes of government. It was the whole set of subjects of the absolutist state in the age of the Leviathan, then that of economic actors in the liberal state. From the viewpoint of the welfare state, it was man himself, with his rights, needs, and labor power, who constituted the basic element of society. What is perverse about the idea of "society" is that it has always helped government to naturalize the product of its activity, its operations, its techniques. It was *constructed as what essentially preexisted it.* It was only after the Second World War, really, that one dared to speak explicitly about "social engineering." Since then, society has officially become what one constructs, sort of like doing nation-building by attacking Iraq. Moreover, this doesn't really work as soon as one openly claims to be doing it.

From era to era, defending society was never anything else but defending the object of government, even when this was being done against those who governed. Up until now, one of the mistakes of revolutionaries has been to fight on the terrain of a fiction that was essentially hostile to them, to appropriate a cause behind which government itself was advancing, wearing a mask. But a good part of our party's current disarray has to do with the fact that, since the 1970s, government has *abandoned this fiction.* It has dropped the idea of integrating all humans into an ordered totality—Margaret Thatcher just had the candor to admit this. In a sense, it has become more pragmatic, and has abandoned the exhausting task of constructing a homogeneous human species that would be well-defined and distinctly separate from the rest of creation, bounded below by things and animals, and above by God, heaven, and the angels. The entry into the era of permanent crisis, the "years of easy money" and the transformation of everyone into desperate entrepreneurs of themselves dealt such a whack to the social idea that it came out of the 1980s somewhat dazed. The next blow, sure to be fatal, consists in the dream of the globalized metropolis, induced by the development of telecommunications and the parceling of the production process on a planetary scale.

One can continue seeing the world in terms of nations and societies, but the latter are now traversed, permeated, by an uncontrollable ensemble of flows. The world presents itself as an immense network in which the large cities, become metropolises, are no longer anything but platforms of interconnection, entry and exit points—*stations*. Henceforth, one can live the same life, it is claimed, in Tokyo or London, in Singapore or New York, with all the metropolises forming one world where what counts is mobility and no longer attachment to a place. Here individual identity serves as a universal *pass* ensuring the possibility, wherever one is, of connecting with the sub-population of one's fellow creatures. But a collection of uber-metropolitans caught up in a constant shuffle from airport terminals to Eurostar toilets doesn't make a society, even a global one. The hyper-bourgeoisie that negociates a contract near the Champs-Élysées before going to hear a set of music on a Rio rooftop and recovers from its emotions with an afterlude at Ibiza symbolizes the decadence of a world—to be enjoyed hastily before it's too late—more than it anticipates any sort of future. Journalists and sociologists cry endlessly over our moribund "society" with their litany about the post-social, the increasing individualism, the disintegration of the old institutions, the loss of reference points, the rise of communalisms, the steady worsening of inequalities. And why wouldn't they, since what is passing away in this case is their livelihood. One will need to think about reinventing oneself.

The revolutionary wave of the years 1960–1970 delivered a fatal blow to the project of a capitalist society into which everyone would integrate peacefully. In response to that, capital undertook a *territorial* restructuring. Since the project of an organized totality was crumbling at its base, it was from there, from secure and interconnected *bases*, plural, that the new global network of value production would be created. It was no longer from "society" that the new form of productivity was expected, but from the territories, from *certain* territories. These last thirty years, capital's restructuring has taken the form of a new spatial ordering of the world. Its focus is the creation of *clusters*, of "centers of innovation," offering "individuals possessing significant social capital"—for the others, sorry, life will be a little more difficult—the best conditions for creating, innovating, and launching, and above all, for doing it collaboratively. The universally recognized model is Silicon Valley. The agents of capital everywhere are getting down to the business of creating an "ecosystem" enabling the individual with the right team to develop fully, to "maximize his talents." This is the new credo of the creative economy—in which the couple engineer/hub of competitiveness is on the dance floor with the duo designer/gentrified neighborhood. According to this new orthodoxy, especially in the Western countries, value production depends on innovation capability. But, as the planners themselves recognize, an environment favorable to creation and its sharing, a productive atmosphere, can't be invented, it is "situated," it sprouts in a place where a history, an identity, can enter into resonance with the spirit of innovation. A *cluster* cannot be imposed, it emerges in a territory on the fertile ground of a "community." If your city is decaying, the solution will not come from investors or the government, explains an entrepreneur who's in fashion. One has to get organized, find other people, get to know each other, work together, recruit other motivated persons, form networks, shake up the status quo... It comes down to the mad dash for a technological advance and the creation of a niche, where the competition is temporarily eliminated and where for a few years one can draw a situational rent. While continuing to think in strategic terms globally, capital deploys a whole casuistry of territorial planning. This allows a bad urbanist to say, concerning the ZAD, a territory under occupation in order to prevent the construction of an airport at Notre-Dame-des-Landes, that it seemed to afford "the opportunity for a kind of Silicon Valley of ecology and society [...] Silicon Valley itself was born in a place that presented little of interest at the time, but where the low cost of space and the mobilization of a few persons contributed to making it the special, internationally acclaimed place it is today." Ferdinand Tönnies, who believed there had never been a society that was not commodity-based, wrote: "Whereas in the *community*, they stay together in spite of everything that separates them, in *society* they remain separate in spite of everything that unites them." In the "creative communities" of capital, people are *bound together by separation itself.* There is no longer any outside from which to distinguish between life and the production of value. Death is in its element. It is young, dynamic, and it smiles at you.

2. The constant incitement to innovate, create, start up, never works so well as on a pile of ruins. Hence all the promotional publicity the past few years around the cool, digital enterprises that are trying to make the industrial desert named Detroit a field of experimentation. "If you think of a city that was near death and that's coming into a new life, it's Detroit. Detroit is a city where something is happening, an open city. What Detroit has to offer is for interested, engaged young people—artists, innovators, musicians, designers, city-makers," writes the man who has oversold the idea of a new urban development articulated around the "creative classes." Yes, he's talking about a city that has lost half its population in fifty years, that has the second highest crime rate of the large American cities, 78,000 abandoned buildings, a former mayor in prison, and whose unofficial unemployment rate approaches 50%—but where Amazon and Twitter have opened new offices. While the fate of Detroit is not yet decided, a promotional operation on the scale of a city has already sufficed to transform a postindustrial disaster lasting several decades, comprising unemployment, depression, illegalities, into a hip district that only swears by culture and technology. It's the same waving of the magical wand that has trans-figured the fair city of Lille since 2004, when it was the ephemeral "European capital of culture."

No need to point out that this involves drastically "renewing" the population of the inner city. From New Orleans to Iraq, what has been aptly called a "shock strategy" makes it possible to obtain, zone by zone, a profitable fragmentation of the world. In this controlled demolition-renovation of "society," the most conspicuous desolation and the most outrageous wealth are just two aspects of the same method of government.

When one reads the prospective reports of the "experts," one finds roughly the following geography: the great metropolitan areas in competition with each other to attract both capital and smart people; the secondary-zone metropolitan poles that manage well enough through specialization; the poor rural zones that cope by becoming places "likely to draw the attention of citizens needing nature and tranquility," zones of agriculture, preferably organic, or "biodiversity preserves"; and lastly, zones of exclusion pure and simple, that will be ringed sooner or later with checkpoints and controlled from a distance with drones, helicopters, swift operations, and massive phone-call interceptions.

So one sees that capital no longer has the problem of "society" but rather that of "governance," as it says politely. Spitting in its face, the revolutionaries of the years 1960–1970 were quite clear that they wanted nothing to do with it. Since then, it selects its people.

Capital doesn't frame itself any longer in national terms, but territory by territory. It doesn't spread itself evenly in very place; it concentrates itself locally by organizing each territory into a milieu of cultivation. It doesn't try to get everyone moving at the same rate, with progress on their radios, but allows the world to delink into zones of intense surplus-value extraction and neglected zones, into theaters of war and pacified spaces. There is the Italian northeast and the Campania, the second just being worthy of receiving the garbage of the first. There is Sofia-Antipolis and Villiers-le-Bel. There is The City and Nottinghill, Tel Aviv and the Gaza strip. The smart cities and the horrible *banlieues*. Ditto for the population. There is no longer a generic "population." There is the young "creative class" that makes its social and relational capital bear fruit in the heart of the smart metropolises, and all those who have so clearly become "unemployable." There are lives that count and others that aren't even factored into the accounts. There is a *plurality* of populations, some being at risk and others having a substantial purchasing power.

If there still remained a cement in the idea of society and a bulwark against its dislocation, it was certainly the hilarious "middle class." All through the 20th century, it went on expanding, at least virtually—so that today two thirds of

Americans and French people sincerely believe they belong to that non-class. But the latter is prey to a pitiless process of selection in its turn. One can't explain the proliferation of reality TV programs staging the most sadistic forms of competition except as a mass propaganda aimed at familiarizing everybody with the little everyday murders among friends that life in a world of constant selection comes down to. According to the oracles of the DATAR, the French governmental agency that plans and coordinates government actions relating to territorial development, in 2040 "the middle class will have shrunk in size," a projection it is pleased about. "The most favored of its members will make up the lowest fraction of the transnational elite," and the others will see "their way of life draw closer to that of the lower classes," that "ancillary army" who will "meet the needs of the elite" and will live in deteriorated districts with an "intellectual proletariat" awaiting integration or estranged from the upper level of the social hierarchy. Put in less opaque terms, their vision is more or less the following: devastated exurban zones, their former inhabitants having moved into the shantytowns to make way for the "metropolitan market gardeners who organize the supply of fresh edible goods to the metropolis over short distances" and the "numerous nature parks," "zones of disconnection," "of recreation for city-dwellers wishing to experience the wild and the unfamiliar."

The degree of likelihood of such scenarios matters little. What counts here is that those claiming to combine future-projection and an action strategy assume the demise of the former society from the outset. The overall dynamic of *selection* contrasts in every particular with the old dialectic of integration, of which social struggles were a moment. The partition between productive territories on one side and distressed territories on the other, between the smart class on one hand and on the other, the "dummies," "retards," "incompetents," those who "resist change" and those who are *attached*, is no longer predetermined by any social organization or cultural tradition. The challenge is to determine *in real time*, in a calibrated way, where the value lies, in which space, with whom, and for what. The reconfigured archipelago of the metropolises has few of the features of the inclusive and hierarchized order called "society." Every totalizing ambition has been abandoned. This is what the DATAR reports show. The same ones who developed the national territory, who constructed the Fordist unity of Gaullist France, have launched themselves into its deconstruction. They announce the "twilight of the nation-state" without regrets. Setting definitive boundaries, whether by establishing sovereign borders or through the unambiguous distinction between man and machine, between man and nature, is a thing of the past. It's the end of the demarcated world. The new metropolitan "society" is distributed over a flat, open, expansive space, not so much smooth as essentially fluid, *runny*. It spreads at its edges, overruns its contours. It's not so easy anymore to say, definitively, who's in and who's out. In the smart world, a smart trash receptacle is much more a part of society than a homeless person or a hick. By re-forming on a horizontal, fragmented, differentiated plane—that of territorial planning and development—and not on the vertical and hierarchical plane derived from medieval theology, "society" as a playing field of government only has vague, shifting, and hence revocable, boundaries. Capital even takes to dreaming of a new "socialism" reserved for its adherents. Now that Seattle has been emptied of its poor people in favor of the futuristic employees of Amazon, Microsoft, and Boeing, the time has come to establish free public transportation there. Surely the city won't go on charging those whose whole life is nothing but value production. That would show a lack of gratitude.

The resolute selection of populations and territories has its own risks. Once the division has been made between those to be supported and those to be allowed to die, it's not certain that those knowing they're destined for the human trash pile will still let themselves be governed. One can only hope to "manage" this cumbersome remainder—assimilating it being unlikely, and liquidating it being indecent no doubt. The planners, whether indifferent or cynical, accept the "segregation," the "increasing inequalities," the "stretching of social hierarchies" as a fact of the times and not as a drift that needs to be halted. The only wayward drift is one that could cause the segregation to morph into a secession—the "flight of a part of the population to peripheries where it might organize into autonomous communities," potentially "at odds with the dominant models of neoliberal globalization." There we have the threat to be managed—but also the way for us to proceed.

We will take on the secession that capital already practices, therefore, but in our own way. Seceding is not carving a part of the territory out of the national whole, it's not isolating oneself, cutting off communications with all the rest—that would be certain death. Seceding is not using the scraps of this world to assemble *counter-clusters* where alternative communities would bask in their imaginary autonomy vis-à-vis the metropolis—that already figures into the plans of the DATAR, which has already foreseen letting them vegetate in their harmless marginality. Seceding means inhabiting a territory, assuming our situated configuration of the world, our way of dwelling there, the form of life and the truths that sustain us, and *from there* entering into conflict or complicity. So it means linking up strategically with other zones of dissidence, intensifying our circulations with friendly regions, regardless of borders. To secede is to break not with the national territory but with the existing geography itself. It's to trace out a different, discontinuous geography, an intensive one, in the form of an archipelago—and thus to go encounter places and territories that are close to us, even if there are 10,000 kilometers to cover. In one of their pamphlets, opponents of the Lyon-Turin rail line write: "What does it mean to be NO TAV? It means to start from a simple statement: 'the high-speed train will never pass through the Susa Valley' and to organize one's life to make it so that this statement is borne out. Many people have come together around this certitude over the past twenty years. On the basis of this quite particular point on which there is no question of yielding, the whole world reconfigures itself. The struggle in the Susa Valley concerns the whole world, not because it is defending the 'common good' in general, but because a certain idea of what is good is commonly thought in the struggle. That idea confronts other notions, defending itself against those wanting to destroy it, and linking up with those having an affinity with it."

3. One of the geopoliticians of territorial development can write that "the increasing intensity of the conflicts around development projects over the past twenty years or so is such that one wonders whether we're not witnessing a gradual shifting of conflictuality in our society from the social to the territorial. As the social struggles have been declining, the struggles over territory have been gaining strength." One is almost tempted to agree, seeing the way the struggle in the Susa Valley has been setting the tempo of political contestation in Italy for several years, from its distant mountains; seeing the consolidating power of the fight against the transport of nuclear waste by the CASTOR trains in Germany's Wendland; and noting the determination of those combating the Hellas Gold mine at Ierissos in Chalkidiki and those who forcibly blocked the construction of a garbage incinerator at Keratea in the Peloponnese. So that more and more revolutionaries are also pouncing on what they call "local struggles" just as greedily as they did on "social struggles" in the past. There are even Marxists who wonder, just a century late, if it might be appropriate to reevaluate the territorial character of so many strikes, so many factory battles that appeared to involve entire regions and not just workers, and the grounds of which may perhaps have been life more than simply the wage relation. The mistake of these revolutionaries is to think of the local in the same way they thought of the working class, as a reality preexisting the struggle. So it is logical for them to imagine that the time had come to build a new international of resistance to the "big useless projects being imposed on us" that would make the resistance stronger and more contagious. This overlooks the fact that, by reconfiguring the everydayness of the territories in struggle, the combat itself creates the consistency of the local, which prior to that was perfectly evanescent. "The movement was not satisfied with defending a 'territory' in the state it found itself in, but inhabited it with thoughts of what it could become [...] It made it exist, constructed it, gave it a consistency," note some opponents of the TAV. Furio Jesi observed that "one gets a better sense of the city during a time of open revolt, with its alternation of charges and counter-charges, than one has playing in the streets as a child, or later walking there with a girl at one's side." It's the same with the inhabitants of the Susa Valley. They wouldn't have such a detailed knowledge of their valley, and such a strong attachment to it, if they had not been fighting for thirty years against the European Union's rotten project.

What is capable of linking these different struggles that *aren't* about "territory" at all, is not the fact of being faced with the same capitalist restructuring, but the ways of living that are invented or rediscovered in the very course of the conflict. What ties them together are the acts of resistance they give rise to—blockage, occupation, riot, sabotage as direct attacks against the production of value through the circulation of information and commodities, through the connection of "innovative territories." The power they generate is not something to be mobilized *with a view to* victory, but victory itself, to the extent that, little by little, the power grows. In this respect, the "Plant your ZAD" movement is well-named. They're in the process of resuming cultivation of the land expropriated by the company contracted to build the Notre-Dame-des-Landes airport, now occupied by inhabitants. An undertaking of this kind immediately places those contemplating it on a long-term basis, longer in any case than that of traditional social movements, and calls for a more general reflection on life at the ZAD and what it can become. A projection that will doubtless include dissemination outside Notre-Dame-des-Landes. In fact, this is already happening in the department of Tarn.

We risk losing everything if we invoke the local as against the global. The local is not the reassuring alternative to globalization, but its universal product. Before the world was globalized, the place I inhabit was simply my familiar territory—I didn't think of it as "local." Local is just the underside of global, its residue, its secretion, and not something capable of shattering it. Nothing was local before one could be pulled away from it at any time, for professional or medical reasons, or for vacation. Local is the name of a possibility of sharing, combined with the sharing of a dispossession. It's a contradiction of the global, which we can give a consistency to or not. Every singular world thus appears for what it is: a fold in *the* world, and not its substantial outside. Reducing to the rather insignificant category of "local struggles"—akin to the pleasantly folkloric "local color"—struggles like those of the Susa Valley, Chalkidiki, or the Mapuche, who have recreated a territory and a people with a planetary aura, is a classic operation of neutralization. For the state, on the pretext that these territories are situated at its margins, it's a matter of marginalizing them politically. Aside from the Mexican state, who would think of categorizing the Zapatista uprising and the adventure that followed from it as a "local struggle"? And yet what could be more localized than that armed insurrection against the thrusts of neoliberalism which inspired a movement of planetary revolt against "globalization," after all. The counter-operation that was successfully carried out by the Zapatistas involved immediately extracting themselves from the national framework, and hence from the minor status of "local struggle," and linking up with all sorts of forces worldwide. In this way they applied their pincer attack to a

Mexican state that was doubly helpless, on its own territory and beyond its borders. The maneuver is unstoppable, and reproducible.

Everything is local, including the global, although we still need to *localize* it. The neoliberal hegemony results from the way it floats in the air, spreads via countless channels that are barely visible for the most part, and appears invincible because it can't be situated. Rather than seeing Wall Street as a celestial raptor dominating the world as God used to, we would have much to gain by determining its material, relational networks, tracking the connections from a trading floor out to their last fiber. One would find, no doubt, that the traders are just idiots, that they don't even deserve their diabolical reputation, but that stupidity is a power in this world. One would ponder those black holes, the clearing houses such as Euronext and Clearstream. Similarly for the state, which is perhaps, as an anthropologist has suggested, nothing more, basically, than a system of personal loyalties. The state is the mafia that has defeated all the others, and has thus won the right to treat them as criminals. To identify this system, trace its contours, locate its vectors, is to restore it to its terrestrial nature, bring it down to its real level. There is research to be done, then, which alone can remove the aura from that which claims hegemony.

Another danger lies in wait for what is expediently construed as "local struggles." Those whose everyday organization shows them the superfluous character of government may imagine that an underlying, prepolitical society exists, where cooperation comes naturally. They are logically induced to position themselves against government in the name of "civil society." But this always entails the postulation of a humanity that is stable, pacified, homogeneous in its positive aspirations, and motivated by a fundamentally Christian disposition to mutual aid, goodness, and compassion. "At the very moment of its triumph," writes an American journalist about the Argentine insurrection of 2001, "the revolution already seems, instantaneously, to have kept its promise: all men are brothers, anyone can speak freely, hearts are full, solidarity is strong. Historically, the formation of a new government transfers much of this power to the state instead of to civil society [...] The period of transition between two regimes seems to be what comes closest to the anarchist ideal of a stateless society, a time when everyone can act and no one holds final authority, when society invents itself as it goes along." A new day would dawn on a responsible humanity full of common sense and capable of taking charge of itself in a respectful and intelligent collaboration. This assumes that the struggle will be content to allow an essentially good human nature to emerge, whereas it's precisely the conditions of struggle that *produce the humanity in question.* The apology of civil society merely reenacts on a global scale the ideal of the passage to adulthood where we could finally do without our guardian, the state, because *we would have finally understood*; we would finally be worthy of self-governance. This litany appropriates everything associated so sadly with becoming an adult: a certain responsible boredom, an overplayed benevolence, the repression of vital affects that inhabit childhood—namely, a certain disposition to play and to conflict. The basic error is doubtless the following: at least since Locke, for the upholders of civil society, "politics" has always meant the tribulations caused by the corruption and negligence of the government—the social base always being natural and without a history. History, precisely, would only be the succession of errors and approximations that delay the coming of a satisfied society into its own. "The great end which men pursue when they enter into society is to enjoy their property peacefully and without danger." Hence those who fight against the government on behalf of "society," whatever their radical claims may be, can only desire, at bottom, to have done with history and the political, which is to say, with the possibility of conflict, which is to say, with *spirited* life.

We start from a very different premise: just as there is no "nature," there is no "society" either. Pulling humans away from all the non-human elements that, for each one of them, go to make up their familiar world, and lumping together the creatures amputated in that way under the name of "society" is a monstrosity that has lasted long enough. Everywhere in Europe there are "communists" or socialists who propose a national way out of the crisis. Their solution would be to leave the euro and constitute a nice limited, homogeneous, and well-ordered totality. These amputees can't keep from hallucinating their phantom member. And of course, as far as nice well-ordered totalities are concerned, the fascists will always have the last word.

No society, then, but *worlds*. And no war against society either: to wage war against a fiction is to give it substance. There's no social sky above our heads, there's us and the ensemble of ties, friendships, enmities, and actual proximities and distances that we experience. There are only sets of us, eminently situated powers, and their ability to ramify throughout the endlessly decomposing and recomposing social carcass. A swarming of worlds, a world made up of a whole slew of worlds, and traversed therefore by conflcts between them, by attractions and repulsions. To construct a world is to create an order, make a place or not for each thing, each being, each proclivity, and give thought to that place, change it if need be. With every manifestation of our party, whether it's in the form of a plaza occupation, a wave of riots, or a deeply moving phrase tagged on a wall, the feeling spreads that it's definitely "we" that's at stake, in all those places where we've never been. This is why the first duty of revolutionaries is to take care of the worlds they constitute. As the Zapatistas have shown, the fact that each world is situated doesn't diminish its access to the generality, but on the contrary is what ensures it. The universal, a poet has said, is the local without the walls. There seems, rather, to be a universalizing potential that is linked to a deepening per se, an intensification of what is experienced in the world at large. It's not a question of choosing between the care we devote to what we are constructing and our political striking force. Our striking force is composed of the very intensity of what we are living, of the joy emanating from it, of the forms of expression invented there, of a collective ability to withstand stresses that is attested by our force. In the general inconsistency of social relations, revolutionaries should stand out by the density of thought, affection, finesse, and organization that they bring to bear, and not by their susceptibility to division and pointless intransigence, or by disastrous competition in the arena of phantasmal radicality.

It's through *attention to the phenomenon*, through their sensitive qualities that they will manage to become a real power, and not through ideological coherence.

Incomprehension, impatience, and negligence are the enemy.

The real is what resists.

Poitiers, Baptistery of St. John, October 10, 2009.

7

OMNIA SUNT COMMUNIA

1. *The Commune Is Coming Back.* **2.** *Inhabiting as a Revolutionary.* **3.** *Defeating the Economy.* **4.** *Taking Part in a Shared Power.*

1. An Egyptian writer, a dyed-in-the-wool liberal, wrote in the now-distant days of the first Tahrir square: "The people I saw on Tahrir Square were new Egyptians, having nothing in common with the Egyptians I was used to dealing with every day. It was as if the revolution had created Egyptians in a higher form […], as if the revolution had not only rid Egyptians of their fear but also cured them of their social defects. […] Tahrir Square became like the Paris Commune. The authority of the regime collapsed and the authority of the people took its place. Committees were formed everywhere, committees to clean the square and committees to set up lavatories and washrooms. Volunteer doctors set up a field hospital." In Oakland, the Occupy movement held Oscar Grant Plaza as the "Oakland Commune." In Istanbul, no better name could be found, already in the first days, than the "Taksim Commune" for what was coming into existence there. A way of saying that revolution was not something that Taksim might lead to one day, but its existence in actuality, its ebullient immanence, here and now. In September, 2012, a poor Nile Delta village, Tahsin, 3,000 inhabitants, declared its independence from the Egyptian state. "We will no longer pay taxes. We will no longer pay for schools. We'll operate our own schools. We'll collect our garbage and maintain our roads ourselves. And if an employee of the state sets foot in the village for any other purpose than to help us, we'll throw him out," they said. In the high mountains of Oaxaca, at the beginning of the 1980s, Indians trying to formulate what was distinctive about their form of life arrived at the notion of "communality." For these Indians, living communally is both what sums up their traditional basis and what they oppose to capitalism, with an "ethical reconstruction of the peoples" in view. In recent years, we've even seen the PKK convert to the libertarian communalism of Murray Bookchin, and project themselves into a federation of communes instead of the construction of a Kurdish state.

Not only is the commune not dead, it is coming back. And it's not returning by chance. It's returning at the very moment the state and the bourgeoisie are fading as historical forces. Now, it was precisely the emergence of the state and the bourgeoisie that put an end to the movement of communalist revolt that shook France from the 11th to the 13th century. The commune, then, is not the chartered town, it's not a collectivity endowed with institutions of self-government. While it can happen that the commune is recognized by this or that authority, generally after battles are fought, it doesn't need that in order to exist. It doesn't always even have a charter, and when there is one, it is quite rare for the latter to stipulate any political or administrative structure. It can have a mayor, or not. What constitutes the commune is the mutual oath sworn by the inhabitants of a city, a town, or a rural area *to stand together as a body*. In the chaos of 11th century France, the commune involved pledging assistance to one another, committing to look out for each other and defend each other against any oppressor. It was literally a *conjuratio*, and such conjurations would have remained an honorable thing if royal jurists had not set about in the following centuries linking them to the idea of conspiracy as a way of getting rid of them. A forgotten historian puts it in a nutshell: "Without association through oath, there would have been no commune, and that association was sufficient for there to be a commune. Commune had exactly the same meaning as common oath." So a commune was a pact to face the world together. It meant relying on one's own shared powers as the source of one's freedom. What was aimed for in this case was not an entity; *it was a qualitative bond, and a way of being in the world.* A pact, then, that couldn't help but implode with the bourgeoisie's monopolization of all the offices and all the wealth, and with the deployment of state hegemony. It was this long-lost, originary, medieval meaning of commune that was somehow rediscovered by the federalist faction of the Paris Commune in 1871. And it's this same meaning that reemerges periodically since that time, from the movement of soviet communes— which was the forgotten spearhead of the Bolshevik revolution till the Stalinist bureaucracy decided to liquidate it—to Huey P. Newton's "revolutionary intercommunalism" by way of the Kwangju Commune of 1980 in South Korea. Declaring the Commune is always to knock historical time off its hinges, to punch a hole in the hopeless continuum of submissions, the senseless succession of days, the dreary struggle of each one to go on living. Declaring the Commune is agreeing to *bond with others*, where nothing will be like it was before.

2. Gustav Landauer wrote: "In the communal life of men there is only one structure appropriate to the space: the commune and the confederation of communes. The borders of the commune make good sense (which naturally excludes disproportion, but not unreason or awkwardness in isolated cases): they delimit a place that ends where it ends." That a political reality can be essentially spatial presents something of a challenge to the modern understanding. First, because we've been accustomed to think of politics as that abstract dimension where positions and discourses are distributed, from left to right. Second, because we inherit from modernity a conception of space as an empty, uniform, and measurable expanse where objects, creatures, or landscapes occupy their place. But the sensible world does not present itself to us in that way. Space is not neutral. Things and beings don't occupy a geometric position, but affect it and are affected by it. Places are irreducibly loaded—with stories, impressions, emotions. A commune engages the world from its own place. Neither an administrative entity nor a simple geometric unit of space, it expresses rather a certain degree of shared experience inscribed territorially. In this way, it adds a depth to the territory which no survey agency can ever represent on any of its maps. By its very existence, it disrupts the reasoned gridding of space, it condemns any vague attempt at "territorial planning" to failure.

The territory of the commune is physical because it is existential. Whereas the forces of occupation conceive of space as a continuous network of *clusters* to which different *branding* operations lend the appearance of diversity, the commune regards itself first of all as a concrete, situated rupture with the overall order of the world. The commune inhabits its territory—that is, it shapes it just as much as the territory offers it a dwelling place and a shelter. It forms the necessary ties there, it thrives on its memory, it finds a meaning, a language, in the land. In Mexico, an Indian anthropologist, one of those defending the "communality" as the guiding principle of their politics, says in reference to the Ayuujk communes: "The community is described as something physical, with the words 'najx' and 'kajp' ('najx,' the land, and 'kajp,' the people). 'Najx,' the land, makes possible the existence of 'kajp,' the people, but the people, 'kajp,' give meaning to the land, 'najx.'" An intensely inhabited territory ends up becoming an affirmation in itself, an articulation, an expression of the life that's lived there. This is seen just as clearly in a Bororo village whose layout makes manifest the inhabitants' relationship with their gods as in the blossoming of tags after a riot, a plaza occupation, any of those occasions when the plebs start inhabiting the urban space again.

The territory is that by which the commune materializes, finds its voice, comes into presence. "The territory is our living space, the stars we see at night, the heat and the cold, the water, the sand, the gravel bars, the forest, our way of being, of working, our music, *our way of talking*." This is a Nahua Indian speaking, one of the *comuneros* who took back—by force of arms, at the end of this century's first decade—the communal lands of Ostula seized by a gang of small landowners of Michoacán. The Nahua went on to declare the autonomous Commune of San Diego de Xayakalan, there on those lands. It seems that every existence with some slight purchase on the world needs a land base for its orientation, whether it's in Seine-Saint-Denis or the Aboriginal lands of Australia. To inhabit is to write each other, to tell one's stories, from a grounded place. This is something we can still hear in the word geography. The territory is to the commune what the word is to the meaning—that is, never just a means. This is what makes the commune and the infinite space of commodity organization the categorical opposites that they are. The territory of the commune is the clay tablet that reveals its meaning as nothing else does, and not a mere expanse endowed with productive functions skillfully distributed by a handful of planning experts. There is as much difference between an inhabited place and a zone of activities as there is between a personal journal and an agenda. Two uses of the land, two uses of ink and paper, with no other resemblance between them.

As a decision to confront the world together, every commune places the world at its center. When a theoretician of communality writes that it "is inherent in the existence and the spirituality of indigenous peoples, characterized by reciprocity, collectivity, kinship ties, primordial loyalties, solidarity, mutual aid, *tequio*, assembly, consensus, communication, horizontality, self-sufficiency, territorial defense, autonomy, and respect for mother earth," he neglects to say that it's the confrontation with our epoch that has required this theorization. The need to autonomize from infrastructures of power is not due to an ageless aspiration to autarky, but has to do with the political freedom that is won in that way. The commune is not preoccupied with its self-definition: what it means to show by materializing is not its identity, not the idea it has of itself, but the idea it has of life. Moreover, the commune can only grow from its outside, as an organism that only lives by internalizing what surrounds it. Precisely because it wants to grow, the commune can only take sustenance from what is not it. As soon as it cuts itself off from the outside, it weakens, devours itself, tears itself apart, loses it vitality, or surrenders to what the Greeks call, with their entire country in mind, "social cannibalism," for the very reason that they feel isolated from the rest of the world. For the commune, there is no difference between gaining in power and concerning itself essentially with what is not it. Historically, the communes of 1871, that of Paris, but also those of Limoges, Périgueux, Lyon, Marseille, Grenoble, Le Creusot, Saint-Étienne, Rouen, as well as the medieval communes, were doomed by their isolation. And just as it was easy, with calm restored in the provinces, for Thiers to come and crush the Parisian proletariat in 1871, in a similar way the main strategy of the Turkish police during the Taksim occupation was to prevent the demonstrations originating in the restive neighborhoods of Gazi and Beşiktaş, or the Anatolian neighborhoods on the other side of the Bosphorus, from rallying to the Taksim cause, and Taksim from forming the link between them. So the paradox facing the commune is the following: it must at the same time succeed in giving some consistency to a territorial reality at odds with the "general order," and it must give rise to, establish links between, local consistencies—that is, it must detach itself from the groundedness that constitutes it. If one of the two objectives is not met, either the commune that's stuck in its own territory becomes gradually isolated and neutralized, or it becomes an itinerant troop, away from home ground, unfamiliar with the situations it passes through, and only inspiring distrust along its way. This is what happened to the detachments of the Long March of 1934. Two thirds of the fighters met their deaths on the journey.

3. That the core of the commune is precisely what eludes it, what traverses it yet always remains beyond its appropriation, was already what characterized the *res communes* in Roman law. The "common things" were the ocean, the atmosphere, the temples, that which could not be appropriated as such. One could take possession of a few liters of water, or a strip of shore, or some temple stones, but not the sea as such, and not a sacred place. The *res communes* are paradoxically what resists reification, their transformation into *res*, into *things*. It's the designation in public law of what falls outside of public law: what's in common use is irreducible to juridical categories. Language is typically "the common": while one can express oneself *thanks to* it, by *means of* it, it is also something which no one can possess as his own. One can only make *use* of it.

In recent years some economists have tried to develop a new theory of the "commons." The "commons" are said to be the set of those things to which the market has a very hard time assigning a value, but without which it would not function: the environment, mental and physical health, the oceans, education, culture, the Great Lakes, etc., but also the great infrastructures (highways, the Internet, telephone or sanitation networks, etc.). According to those economists, who are both worried about the state of the planet and desirous of improving the operation of the market, there needs to be invented a new form of "governance" for these commons that wouldn't depend on the market alone. *Governing the Commons* is the title of the recent bestseller by Elinor Ostrom, Nobel Prize in Economics in 2009, who has defined eight principles for "managing the commons." Understanding there is a place for them in an "administration of the commons" that remains to be invented, Negri and associates have embraced this theory, which is perfectly liberal at its core. They've even extended the notion of commons to include everything produced by capitalism, reasoning that all of it results in the last analysis from the productive collaboration between humans, who would only need to appropriate it through an uncommon "democracy of the commons." The eternal militants, always short of ideas, have rushed into step behind them. They now find themselves claiming "health, housing, migration, social care, education, working conditions in the textile industry, etc." as so many "commons" that must be appropriated. If they continue down this path, it won't be long before they demand worker management of nuclear power plants and the same for the NSA, since the

Internet should belong to everyone. For their part, more sophisticated theoreticians are inclined to make the "commons" into the latest metaphysical principle to come out of the West's magical hat. An *arche*, they say, in the sense of that which "organizes, commands, and rules all political activity," a new "beginning" that will give birth to new institutions and a new world government. What is ominous about all this is the evident inability to imagine any other form of revolution than the existing world flanked by an administration of men and things inspired by the ravings of Proudhon and the lackluster fantasies of the Second International. Contemporary communes don't claim any access to, or aspire to the management of any "commons." They immediately organize a shared form of life— that is, they develop a *common relationship* with what cannot be appropriated, beginning with the world.

If ever these "commons" were to pass into the hands of a new breed of bureaucrats, nothing about what is killing us would substantially change. The entire *social* life of the metropolises works like a gigantic demoralization enterprise. Everyone within it, in every aspect of their existence, is *held captive* by the general organization of the commodity system. One can very well be activist in one organization or another, go out with one's group of "buddies," but ultimately it's everybody for themselves, each in his own skin, and there's no reason to think it might be different. Every movement, however, every genuine encounter, every episode of revolt, every strike, every occupation, is a breach opened up in the false self-evidence of *that life*, attesting that a *shared* life is possible, desirable, potentially rich and joyful. It sometimes seems that everything is conspiring to prevent us from believing this, to obliterate every trace of other forms of life— of those that died out and those about to be eradicated. The desperate ones at the helm of the ship are most afraid of having passengers less nihilistic than they are. And indeed, the entire organization of this world, that is, of our strict dependence on it, is a daily denial of every other possible form of life.

As the social varnish cracks and peels, the urgency of forming into a force is spreading, under the surface but noticeably. Since the end of the movement of the squares, we have seen networks of mutual support cropping up in many cities to stop evictions, of strike committees and neighborhood assemblies, but also cooperatives, for everything and in every sense. Production co-ops, consumer co-ops, housing, education, and credit co-ops, and even "integral co-ops" that would deal with every aspect of life. With this proliferation, a welter of previously marginal practices is spreading far beyond the radical ghetto that had more or less reserved them for itself. In this way they're acquiring a seriousness and effectiveness that wasn't there before, and they themselves are easier to deal with. Not everyone is alike. People are facing the need for money together, they're organizing to have some or do without. And yet, a cooperative wood shop or auto repair shop will be just as irksome as a paying job if they're taken as the aim instead of the means that people have in common. Every economic entity is headed for oblivion, is oblivion *already*, if the commune doesn't negates its claim to completeness. So the commune is what brings all the economic communities into communication with each other, what runs through and overflows them; it is the link that thwarts their self-centering tendency. The ethical fabric of the Barcelona workers' movement at the beginning of the 20th century can serve as a guide for the experiments that are underway. What gave it its revolutionary character was not its libertarian schools or its small operators who printed contraband money stamped CNT-FAI, or its sectoral trade unions, or its workers' co-ops, or its groups of *pistoleros*. It was the *bond* connecting all this, the life flourishing *between* all these activities and entities, and not assignable to any of them. This was its unassailable base. It's noteworthy, moreover, that at the time of the insurrection of July 1936 the only ones capable of tying together all the components of the anarchist movement offensively was the group Nosotros: a marginal bunch whom the movement had suspected up to that point of "anarcho-Bolshevism," and who a month earlier had undergone a public trial and a quasi-exclusion on the part of the FAI.

In several European countries hit by "crisis," we're seeing an emphatic return of the social and solidarity-based economy, and of the cooperativist and mutualist ideologies that accompany it. The idea is spreading that this might constitute an "alternative to capitalism." We see it rather as an alternative to struggle, an alternative *to the commune*. To convince oneself of this, one only has to look at how the social and solidarity economy was utilized by the World Bank, particularly in South America, as a technique of political pacification over the last twenty years. It's well known that the noble project of helping the "Third World" countries to develop was conceived in the 1960s in the notably counter-insurrectionary mind of Robert McNamara, the US Secretary of Defense from 1961 to 1968, the McNamara of Vietnam, Agent Orange, and Rolling Thunder. The essence of this economic project is not in any way economic: it's purely political, and its principle is simple. To guarantee the "security" of the United States, that is, to defeat communist insurrections, one has to deprive them of their main cause: excessive poverty. No poverty, no insurrection. Pure Galula. "The security of the Republic," wrote McNamara in 1968, "doesn't depend exclusively, or even primarily, on its military might, but also on the creation of stable economic and political systems, as much here at home as in the developing countries all over the world." From such a viewpoint, the fight against poverty has several things going for it: first, it makes it possible to hide the fact that the real problem is not poverty, but wealth— the fact that a few hold, together with their power, most of the means of production; further, it turns the problem into a question of social engineering and not a political issue. Those who make fun of the near-systematic failure of the World Bank's interventions to reduce poverty, from 1970 on, would do well to note that for the most part they were clear successes *in terms of their true goal*: preventing insurrection. This excellent run was to last until 1994.

1994 was when the National Program of Solidarity (PRONOSOL) was launched in Mexico with the support of 170,000 local "solidarity committees" designed to soften the effects of brutal social destructuring that would logically be produced by the free-trade agreements with the United States. It led to the Zapatista insurrection. Since then, the World Bank is all about microcredit, "reinforcing the autonomy and *empowerment* of poor people" (World Development Report of 2001), cooperatives, mutual societies—in short: the social and solidarity economy. "Promote the mobilization of poor people into local organizations so they can act as a check on the state institutions, participate in the process of local decision-making, and thus collaborate to ensure the primacy of law in everyday life," says the same report. Meaning: co-opt the local leaders into our networks, neutralize the oppositional groups, enhance the value of "human capital," bring into commodity circuits, even marginal ones, everything that escaped them previously. The integration of tens of thousands of cooperatives, even rehabilitated factories, into the program Argentina Trabaja, is the counter-insurrectionary masterwork of Cristina Kirchner, her calibrated response to the uprising of 2001. Not to be outdone, Brazil has its own National Secretariat of Solidarity Economy, which in 2005 already counted 15,000 businesses and is a fine addition to the success story of local capitalism. The "mobilization of civil society" and the development of a "different economy" are not an adjusted response to the "shock strategy," as Naomi Klein naively thinks, but the other stroke of its mechanism. The enterprise-form, the alpha and omega of neoliberalism, spreads along with the cooperatives. One should not be overly pleased, as some Greek leftists are, that the number of self-managed co-ops has exploded in their country these last two years. Because the World Bank keeps exactly the same tallies, and with the same satisfaction. The existence of a responsive marginal economic sector of the social and solidarity type doesn't pose any threat to the concentration of political, hence economic, power. It even protects it from every challenge. Behind such a defensive buffer, the Greek ship-owners, the army, and the country's large corporations can go on with their business as usual. A bit of nationalism, a touch of social and solidarity economy, and the insurrection will have to wait.

Before economics could claim the title of "the science of behaviours," or even the status of "applied psychology," the economic creature, the being of need, had to be made to proliferate on the surface of the Earth. This being of need, this needy toiler, is not a creation of nature. For a long time, there were only ways of living, and not needs. One inhabited a certain portion of this world and one knew how to feed oneself, clothe oneself, entertain oneself, and put a roof over one's head there. Needs were his-torically produced, by tearing men and women away from their world. Whether this took took the form of raids, expropriation, enclosures, or colo-nization matters little in this context. Needs were what economy gave to man in return for the world it took away. We start from that premise, there's no use denying it. But if the commune involves taking responsibility for needs, this is not out of a concern for autarky, but because economic dependence on this world is a political as much as existential cause of continual abasement. The commune addresses needs with a view to annihilating the being of need within us. Where a lack is felt, its elementary gesture is to find the means to make it disappear as often as it may present itself. There are those "in need of a house"? One doesn't just build one for them; one sets up a workshop where anyone can quickly build a house for themselves. A place is needed for meeting, hanging-out, or partying? One is occupied or built and also made available to those who "don't belong to the commune." The question, as you can see, is not that of abundance, but of the disappearance of need, that is, participation in a collective power that can dispel the feeling of confronting the world alone. The intoxication of the movement is not enough for this; a profusion of *means* is required. So a distinction must be made between the recent restarting of the Vio.Me factory in Thessaloniki by its workers and a number of variously disastrous Argentine attempts at self-management which Vio.Me takes inspiration from nonetheless. What is different is that the resumption of factory production was conceived from the beginning as a political offensive supported by all the remaining elements of the Greek "movement," and not merely as an attempt at alternative economy. Using the same machines, this factory producing tile-joint compounds was converted to the production of disinfectant gels that were supplied in particular to dispensaries operated by the "movement." It's the echo made here *between* several facets of the "movement," which has a communelike character. If the commune "produces," this can only be in an incidental way; if it satisfies our "needs," this is something extra as it were, in addition to its desire for a shared life; and not by taking productions and needs as the object. It's in the open offensive against this world that the commune will find the allies that its growth demands. The growth of communes is the real crisis of economy, and is the only serious degrowth.

4. A commune can be formed in any situation, around any "problem." The workers of the AMO factories, pioneers of Bolshevik communalism, opened the first communal house of the USSR because after years of civil war and revolution, they were sorely lacking in places to go for vacation. A communard wrote this, in 1930: "And when the long rains of autumn began to beat down on the roof of the collective dacha, under that roof a firm decision was made: we would continue our experiment during the winter." If there's no privileged starting point for the birth of a commune, it's because there's no privileged point of entry into the epoch. Every situation, if it's engaged with in a focused way, brings us back to this world and links us to it, to its unbearable aspects as well as the cracks and openings it presents. In each detail of existence, the entire form of life is at stake. Because the object of every commune is the world, basically,

the commune must be careful not to let itself be completely determined by the task, the question, or the situation that led to its formation and were only the *occasion* of the convergence. Thus, in a commune's unfolding, a good threshold is crossed when the desire to be together and the power that comes from that outstrip the initial reasons for its formation.

If in the course of the recent uprisings there was one thing conveyed by the streets, beyond the dissemination of riot techniques and the now-universal use of gas masks—that symbol of an epoch that's become unbreathable—it was the initiation into joy that's equivalent to a whole political education. Over these last few years, there was no one, not even the shaved-neck assholes of Versailles, who didn't develop a taste for the wild demonstration and the ruckus with the cops. Each time, the situations of urgency, riot, occupation gave rise to more than was committed to them initially in terms of demands, strategy, or hope. Those who went to Taksim to prevent six hundred trees from being ripped out soon found something else to defend: the square itself, as a matrix and expression of a power regained at last, after ten years of political castration and preventive dismemberment of every semblance of collective organization.

What partakes of the commune in the occupation of Tahrir Square, the Puerta del Sol, or some American occupations, or in the forty unforgettable days of the Free Republic of Maddalena in the Susa Valley, is discovering that one can organize in so many domains that they can't be totalized. This is what exhilarated us: the feeling of taking part in, of experiencing, a shared power, one that was unassignable and fleetingly invulnerable. Invulnerable because the joy that haloed each moment, each gesture, each encounter, could *never* be taken away from us. Who's cooking meals for a thousand persons? Who's doing the radio? Who's writing the communiqués? Who's catapulting rocks at the cops? Who's building a house? Who's cutting wood? Who's speaking in the assembly? We don't know, and don't give a fuck: all of that is a *force with no name*, as a Spanish Bloom said, borrowing the notion without knowing it from the 14th century heretics of the Free Spirit. Only the fact of sensing that what one is doing, what one is living through, participates in a spirit, a force, a richness shared in common will enable us to be done with economy, that is, with calculation, measurement, with evaluation, with all that petty accountant's mentality which is everywhere the mark of resentment, in love as well as in the workshops. A friend who had been camping for a long spell on Syntagma Square did a double take when he was asked how the Greeks would have been able to organize their food supply if the movement had burned down the Parliament and brought down the country's economy in a definitive way: "Ten million persons have never let themselves die of hunger. Even if that might have caused a few skirmishes here and there, the disorder would have been tiny compared to the disorder that's ordinarily the case."

What characterizes the *situation* that a commune faces is that by giving oneself to it unreservedly, one always finds more in it than one brought to it or sought from it: one is surprised to find one's own strength in it, a stamina and an inventiveness that is new, plus the happiness that comes from strategically inhabiting a situation of exception on a daily basis. In this sense, *the commune is the organization of fertility*. It always gives rise to more than it lays claim to. This is what makes *irreversible* the unheaval that affected the crowds that descended on all the squares and avenues of Istanbul. Crowds forced for weeks to deal on their own with the crucial questions of provisioning, construction, care and treatment, burial, or armament not only learned to organize themselves, but learned something that most didn't know: that we *can* organize ourselves, and that this capacity is fundamentally joyful. The fact that this fertility of the street was not mentioned by any of the democratic commentators is a rather clear indication of its dangerous potential. The memory of those days and nights makes the orderly everydayness of the metropolis appear even more intolerable, and exposes its pointlessness.

Sirte, October 2011.

8

TODAY LIBYA, TOMORROW WALL STREET

1. *A History of Fifteen Years.* 2. *Pulling Free from the Attraction of the Local.* 3. *Building a Force That Is Not an Organisation.* 4. *Taking Care of Our Power.*

1. On July 3, 2011, in response to the eviction of the Maddalena, tens of thousands of persons converged in several columns on the construction site, occupied by the police and the army. That day, in the Susa Valley, there was a real battle. A somewhat adventurous *carabiniere* was even captured and disarmed by some demonstrators in the *boschi*, the woods. From the hairdresser to the grandmother, nearly everybody had equipped themselves with a gas mask. Those too old to go out cheered us on from the doorways of their houses, with words like *"Ammazzateli!"*—"Kill them!" In the end, the occupation forces were not dislodged from their nook. And the next day, the

newspapers repeated the police's lies in unison: "Maalox and ammonia: the Black Bloc guerilla," and so forth. As a riposte to this propaganda via slander, a press conference was called. The movement's response included this: "Well, all right, if attacking the construction site makes you a Black Bloc, then we're all Black Blocs!" Ten years earlier, almost day for day, the servile press had served up the same explanation for the battle of Genoa: the Black Bloc, an entity of indeterminate origin, had managed to infiltrate the demonstration and wreak bloody havoc on the city, all by itself. The public discourse pitted the demonstration's organizers, who defended the theory that the said Black Bloc was actually composed of plainclothes policemen, against those who saw them as a terrorist organization based in a foreign country. The least one can say is that the policing rhetoric has stayed exactly what it was, while the real movement has covered some ground.

From our party's perspective, a strategic reading of the past fifteen years must start with the anti-globalization movement, the last worldwide offensive organized against capital. It makes little difference whether we date its inception from the Amsterdam demonstration against the Maastricht Treaty in 1997, the Geneva riots in May 1998 against the WTO, the London Carnival Against Capital in June 1999 or the one in Seattle in

November of the same year. Nor does it matter much whether one considers that it survived the Genoa climax and was still alive in 2007 at Heiligendam or at Toronto in June 2010. What is certain is that at the end of the 1990s there emerged a planetary movement of critique targeting multinationals and global organs of government (IMF, World Bank, European Union, G8, NATO, etc.). The global counterrevolution that cited September 11 as its justification should be understood as a political response to the anti-globalization movement. After Genoa, the crack that was visible in the very framework of "Western societies" had to be covered over by every available means. Logically, in the autumn of 2008, the "crisis" emanated from the very heart of the capitalist order, from the privileged target of the "anti-globalization" critique. The fact is that counterrevolution, however massive it may be, only has the power to freeze the contradictions, not eradicate them. Just as logically, what returned at that juncture was what had been brutally repressed for seven years. A Greek comrade summed it up in this way: "In December 2008, it was Genoa on the scale of a whole country and lasting for a month." The contradictions had been ripening under the ice.

Historically, the anti-globalization movement will remain as the first attack of the planetary petty bourgeoisie against capital—a touching and ineffectual one, like a premonition of its coming proletarization. There's not a single historical occupation of the petty bourgeoisie—doctor, journalist, lawyer, artist, or teacher—that hasn't been changed into an activist version: street medic, alternative reporter for Indymedia, legal team, or specialist in solidarity economics. The evanescent nature of the anti-globilization movement, volatile down to its counter-summit riots, where a club raised in the air was enough to excite a crowd like a flock of sparrows, has to do with the floating character of the petty bourgeoisie itself, with its historical indecision, its political nullity, as a non-class of the space between two classes. The paucity of reality of the one explains the paucity of resistance of the other. The winter winds of counterrevolution were enough to quell the movement, in a few seasons.

If the soul of the anti-globalization movement was its critique of the global apparatus of government, we can say that the "crisis" expropriated the custodians of that critique: the militants and activists. What was obvious to the limited circles of politicized creatures is now flagrantly evident to everyone. Since the autumn of 2008, never has it made more sense, and such a widely-shared sense, to smash banks, but precisely for that reason, so little sense to do it in a small group of professional rioters. Since 2008, it's as if the anti-globalization movement has dissolved into reality. It has disappeared, precisely because it has been realized. Everything that constituted its basic vocabulary has entered the public domain, so to speak. Who still doubts the impudent "dictatorship of finance," the political function of the restructurings ordered by the IMF, the devastation of the environment by capitalist rapacity, the insane arrogance of the nuclear lobby, the reign of the most brazen lies and blatant corruption of the rulers? Who is not flabbergasted by the unilateral consecration of neoliberalism as the remedy for its own failure? We need to remember how the convictions forming common opinion today were restricted to militant circles ten years ago.

The anti-globalization movement even saw its own arsenal of practices looted by "people." The Puerta del Sol had its Legal Team, its Medical Team, its Info point, its hacktivists, and its camping tents, just like any counter-summit or "No Border" camp did in years past. What was introduced into the heart of the Spanish capital were forms of assembly, an organization into *barrios* and committees, and even ridiculous gestural codes that all came from the anti-globalization movement. Early in the morning of June 15, 2011, the campers, numbering in the thousands, tried to blockade the Catalonia parliament to prevent it from approving the "austerity plan," just as the demonstrators stopped the different countries' IMF representatives from entering the conference center a few years before. The book blocs of the English student movement of 2011 were the resumption in a "social movement" setting of a Tute Bianche practice in the counter-summits. On February 22, 2014 at Nantes, during the demonstration against the airport project, the riot practice of acting in small masked mobile groups was so generalized that to speak of a "Black Bloc" was no longer anything but a way of reducing what was new to the already-known, when it wasn't just the language of the Minister of the Interior. In situations where the police only discern the action of "radical groups," it's not hard to see that they're trying to conceal a general radicalization.

2. Thus, our party is everywhere, but it's at a standstill. With the disappearance of the anti-globalization movement, the perspective of a movement as planetary as capital itself, and hence capable of doing battle with it, was lost as well. So the first question we are faced with is the following: how does a set of situated powers constitute a global force? How does a set of communes constitute a historical party? Or to put it differently: it was necessary at a certain point to abandon the

ritual of counter-summits with its professional activists, its depressive puppetmasters, its predictable riots, its plenitude of slogans and its dearth of meanings, and attach ourselves to lived territories; we had to tear ourselves away from the abstraction of the global. The question at present is how do we tear ourselves away from *the attraction of the local*?

Traditionally, revolutionaries expect the unification of their party to come from the naming of the common enemy. It's their incurable dialectical defect. "Dialectical logic," said Foucault, "brings contradictory terms into play in a homogeneous context. I suggest replacing this dialectical logic with what I would call strategic logic. A logic of strategy doesn't stress contradictory terms operating within a homogeneity that promises their resolution into a unity. The function of strategic logic is to establish the possible connections between disparate terms that remain disparate. The logic of strategy is the logic of connections between the heterogeneous and not the logic of the homogenization of the contradictory."

No effective link between communes, between heterogeneous, situated powers will result from the designation of a common enemy. If, in the forty years they have debated, militants still have not decided whether the enemy is alienation, exploitation, capitalism, sexism, racism, civilization, or in fact what exists in its entirety, it's because the question as it is formulated is basically vacuous. The enemy is not simply something that can be designated once we've detached ourselves from all our determinations, once we've transported ourselves to who knows what political or philosophical plane. From the standpoint of such a detachment, all cats are grey, the real is bathed in the very strangeness that we've brought upon ourselves: all is hostile, cold, indifferent. The militant can then sally forth against this or against that, but it will always be against a form of emptiness, a form *of his own emptiness*—powerlessness and windmills. For anyone who *starts from where they are*, from the milieu they frequent, the territory they inhabit, the frontline defines itself, based on the matter at hand, *the contact*. Who is working for the dirtbags? Who's afraid of getting involved? Who will take risks for what they believe in? How far will the opposing party allow itself to go? What does it back away from? What does it rely upon? It's not a unilateral decision but experience itself that outlines the response to these questions, from situation to situation, from encounter to encounter. Here the enemy is not that ectoplasm that is constituted by naming it; the enemy is what *presents itself*, what imposes itself on all those who aren't attempting to shed what they are and where they are and project themselves onto the abstract terrain of politics—that desert. Although it only presents itself to those with enough life in them not to instinctively flee from conflict.

Every declared commune calls a new geography into existence around it, and sometimes even at a distance from it. Where there had only been a uniform territory, a plain where everything was interchangeable, in the greyness of generalized equivalence, it raises up a chain of mountains, a whole variegated relief with passes, peaks, incredible pathways between friendly things, and forbidding precipitous terrain between enemy things. Nothing is simple anymore, or is simple in a different way. Every commune *creates* a political territory that extends out and ramifies as it grows. It is in this movement that it marks out the paths leading to other communes, that it forms the lines and links making up our party. Our strength won't come from our naming of the enemy, but from the effort made to enter one another's geography.

We're the orphans of a time when the world was falsely divided into agents and enemies of the capitalist bloc. With the collapse of the Soviet illusion, every simple grid of geopolitical interpretation was lost. No ideology enables us *from afar* to separate friends from enemies—notwithstanding the desperate attempt to instate a newly reassuring reading grid where Iran, China, Venezuela or Bashar al-Assad look like heroes of the struggle against imperialism. Who could have determined *from here* the exact nature of the Libyan insurrection? Who can sort out, in the occupation of Taksim, what falls under the old Kemalism and what is due to the aspiration for a new world? And Maidan? What does one say about Maidan? One would have to go see. One would have to go make contact. And in the complexity of the movements, to discern the shared friends, the possible alliances, the necessary conflicts. According to a logic of strategy, and not of dialectics.

"From the start," wrote our comrade Deleuze more than forty years ago, "we have to be more centralist than the centralists. Clearly, a revolutionary machine can't be satisfied with local and limited struggles: it has to be super-centralized and super-desiring at the same time. The problem, then, concerns the nature of unification, which must function transversally, through multiplicity, not vertically and not in such a way that the multiplicity characterizing desire will be crushed." As long as ties exist between us, the scatteredness, the fragmented cartography of our party is not a weakness, but rather a way of depriving the hostile forces of any decisive target. As a friend from Cairo put it in the summer of 2010: "I think that what may have saved what has happened in Egypt up to now is that there's no leader of this revolution. That may be the most disconcerting thing for the police, for the state, for the government. There's no head to cut off to make this thing stop. Like a virus constantly mutating to preserve its existence, it's this way we've had of preserving the popular organization, without any hierarchy, completely horizontal, organic, and diffuse." Morever, what is not structured like a state, like an organization, can only be scattered and fragmentary, and discovers the very motive force of its expansion in this constellated form. It's up to us to organize the encounters, the circulation, the understandings, the collusions between the local consistencies. The revolutionary task has partly become a task of translation. There is no Esperanto of revolt. It's not up to the rebels to learn to speak anarchist; it's up to the anarchists to become polyglot.

3. We are faced with this difficulty: how does one construct a force that is not an organization? Here again, the question must have been badly formulated since it received no satisfactory answer during a century of quarreling on the theme of "spontaneity or organization." This false problem stems from a blindness, an inability to perceive the organizational forms implied by the

term "spontaneous." Every life, let alone every shared life, secretes ways of being, of speaking, of producing, of loving, of fighting, regularities therefore, customs, a language—forms. The thing is, we have learned not to see forms in what is alive. For us, a form is a statue, a structure, or a skeleton, and never a being that moves, eats, dances, sings, and riots. Real forms are immanent in life and can only be apprehended in motion. An Egyptian comrade gave us this account: "Cairo was never more alive than during the first Tahrir Square. Since nothing was functioning anymore, everyone took care of what was around them. People took charge of the garbage collecting, swept the walkways and sometimes even repainted them; they drew frescos on the walls and they looked after each other. Even the traffic had become miraculously fluid, since there were no more traffic controllers. What we suddenly realized is that we had been robbed of our simplest gestures, those that make the city ours and make it something we belong to. At Tahrir Square, people would arrive and spontaneously ask themselves what they could do to help. They would go to the kitchen, or to stretcher the wounded, work on banners or shields or slingshots, join discussions, make up songs. We realized that the state organization was actually the maximum disorganization, because it depended on negating the human ability to self-organize. At Tahrir, no one gave any orders. Obviously, if someone had got it in their heads to organize all that, it would have immediately turned into chaos." One is reminded of the famous letter written by Courbet during the Commune: "Paris is a real paradise: no police, no nonsense, no abuse of any kind, no quarrels. Paris is cruising by itself, like something on wheels. If only we could stay like this forever. In a word, it's a real enchantment." From the collectivizations of Aragon in 1936 to the occupations of squares in recent years, personal accounts of the same enchantment are a constant of History; the war of all against all is not what comes when the state is no longer there, but what the state skillfully organizes for as long as it exists.

And yet, recognizing the forms that life spontaneously engenders does not mean that we can rely on some kind of spontaneity to maintain those forms and foster their growth, to bring about the necessary metamorphoses. On the contrary, that requires a constant attention and discipline. Not the reactive, cybernetic, punctual attention that is shared by activists and the management vanguard, who only swear by networks, fluidity, feedback, and horizontality, who manage everything without understanding anything, from the outside. Not the external, vaguely military discipline of the old organizations spawned by the workers' movement, which have almost all become appendices of the state, it should be said. The attention and the discipline we have in mind is directed towards our power, towards its condition, and its increase. They watch for signs of anything encroaching on it, and figure out what makes it grow. They never mistake a letting-go—that bane of communes—for a letting-be. They take care that everything isn't mixed together on the pretext of sharing everything. They're not the prerogative of a few, but the entitlement of everyone to initiative. They're both the precondition and the object of real sharing, and its gauge of subtlety. They're our protection against the tyranny of the informal. They're the very texture of our party. In forty years of neoliberal counter-revolution, it's first of all this link between discipline and joy that's been forgotten. It's now being rediscovered. True discipline isn't focused on the external signs of organization, but on the internal development of our power.

4. The revolutionary tradition is stamped with voluntarism as if it were a congenital defect. Living strained towards the future, marching towards victory, is one of the few ways to endure a present whose horror one can't conceal from oneself. Cynicism is another option, the worst one, the most banal. A revolutionary force of this

era will attend instead to the patient growth of its power. This question having long been pushed back, behind the antiquated theme of seizing power, we're relatively unprepared when the moment comes to address it. There's never a lack of bureaucrats who know exactly what they intend to do with the power of our movements, that is, how they intend to make it a means, a means *to their end*. But we don't usually concern ourselves with our power as such. We sense that it exists, we perceive its fluctuations, but we treat it with the same casualness we reserve for anything "existential." A certain illiteracy in the matter isn't incompatible with the bad texture of radical milieus: engaged as it is in a pathetic competition for miniscule shares of the political market, every little groupuscular enterprise foolishly believes that it will come out stronger for having weakened its rivals by slandering them. This is a mistake: one increases in power by combating an enemy, not by demeaning him. The cannibal himself is better than that: if he eats his enemy, it's because he esteems him enough to want to feed on his strength.

Not being able to draw from the revolutionary tradition on this point, we can appeal to comparative mythology. We know that in his study of Indo-European mythologies, Dumézil was led to his famous tripartition: "Beyond the priests, the warriors, and the producers, there were the corresponding hierarchized 'functions' of magical and juridical sovereignty, physical and mainly warlike strength, peaceful and fertile abundance." Let's leave aside the hierarchy between "functions" and speak of dimensions instead. We'll say this: every power in our sense has three dimensions—spirit, force, and richness. Its growth depends on keeping the three of them together. As a historical power, a revolutionary movement is that deployment of a spiritual expression—which may take a theoretical, literary, artistic, or metaphysical form—of a war-making capacity—which may be oriented towards attack or towards self-defense—and of an abundance of material means and places. These three dimensions are variously combined in time and space, giving rise to forms, dreams, forces, and histories that are always singular. But whenever one of these dimensions loses contact with the others and becomes independent of them, the movement has degenerated. It has degenerated into an armed vanguard, a sect of theoreticians, or an alternative enterprise. The Red Brigades, the Situationists, and the nightclubs— sorry, the "social centers"—of the Disobedients are standard formulas of failure as far as revolution goes. Ensuring an increase of power demands that every revolutionary force progress on each of these planes simultaneously. To remain stuck on the offensive plane is eventually to run out of cogent ideas and to make the abundance of means insipid. To stop moving theoretically is a sure way of being caught off guard by the movements of capital and of losing the ability to apprehend life as it's lived where we are. To give up on constructing worlds with our hands is to resign oneself to a ghostly existence.

A friend wrote: "What is happiness? It's the feeling that our power *is increasing*—that an obstacle is being overcome."

To become revolutionary is to assign oneself a difficult, but immediate, happiness.

We would have liked to be brief. To forgo genealogies, etymologies, quotations. That a poem, a song, would suffice.

We wished it would be enough to write "revolution" on a wall for the street to catch fire.

But it was necessary to untangle the skein of the present, and in places to settle accounts with ancient falsehoods.

It was necessary to try and digest seven years of historical convulsions. And decipher a world in which confusion has blossomed on a tree of misunderstanding.

We've taken the time to write with the hope that others would take the time to read.

Writing is a vanity, unless it's for the friend. Including the friend one doesn't know yet.

In the coming years, we'll be wherever the fires are lit.

During the periods of respite, we're not that hard to find.

We'll continue the effort of clarification we've begun here.

There will be dates and places where we can mass our forces against logical targets.

There will be dates and places for meeting up and debating.

We don't know if the insurrection will have the look of a heroic assault, or if it will be a planetary fit of crying, a sudden expression of feeling after decades of anesthesia, misery, and stupidity.

Nothing guarantees that the fascist option won't be preferred to revolution.

We'll do what there is to be done.

Thinking, attacking, building—such is our fabulous agenda.

This text is the beginning of a plan.

See you soon,

Invisible Committee
October 2014

semiotext(e) intervention series